The BLOOD of The

CU00969927

Introduction: The BLOOD of The C

This lesson will focus on the PURPOSE (Savior, because there are doctrines among ᴜᴄ ᴴᴇᴏrews that give them the impression that the Blood of Christ free them from SIN, from breaking the LAW.

1 John 3:4 Whosoever committeth sin transgresseth also the law: for sin is the transgression of the law.

If you think The Most High God of Abraham, Isaac, and Jacob sent His Son to VOID out His Laws, that is absurd!

Hebrews 10:26 For if we sin willfully after that we have received the knowledge of the truth, there remaineth no more sacrifice for sins,

Let me explain this, for those who may not understand. If you know sleeping with another man's wife is a SIN, but you do it anyway, or you know stealing and killing is a SIN, but you continue to commit it and afterwards, pray for forgiveness, Christ did not sacrifice His BLOOD to cover willful sin.

Hebrews 10:29 Of how much sorer punishment, suppose ye, shall he be thought worthy, who hath trodden underfoot the Son of God, and hath counted the blood of the covenant, wherewith he was sanctified, an unholy thing, and hath done despite unto the Spirit of grace?

Those who are willfully SINNING in this manner, you are stepping on the BLOOD of Christ, disrespecting His SACRIFICE, that he died for you, and you are TREADING over the Laws of His Father. What kind of charlatan gave you this RELIGION?

Romans 6:1 What shall we say then? Shall we continue in sin, that grace may abound?

Apostle Paul asked this question: should you continue to sin because you have GRACE?

The BLOOD of The Covenants

Romans 6:2 God forbid. How shall we, that are dead to sin, live any longer therein?

The answer is "NO!" When you are under Grace, you have REPENTED, and RETURNED to the Law and you have learned the Law.

Titus 2:11 For the grace of God that bringeth salvation hath appeared to all men,

Grace of The Most High God SAVE you! We will go into details later.

Titus 2:12 Teaching us that, denying ungodliness and worldly lusts, we should live soberly, righteously, and godly, in this present world;

When you are under GRACE, you have REPENTED, and are LEARNING the Law. You are DENYING SIN, not sinning then saying that you are under GRACE. A REPENTANT Israelite is practicing RIGHTEOUS living, and when you fall, GRACE is there to catch you. From this perspective, you are NOT under GRACE unless you have REPENTED and RETURNED to the Law.

The BLOOD of The Covenants

Table of Contents

The BLOOD of The Covenants

The BLOOD of The Covenants

The BLOOD of The Covenants

The BLOOD of The Covenants

Chapter 1: The Old Covenant

Let me begin with the First Covenant, or Old Testament. I will show you who the First Covenant belonged and the purpose of the BLOOD of LAMBS, and GOATS.

Who Does the Old Covenant Belongs?
We need to begin at this interval, because it becomes relevant when we get to the New Covenant.

Genesis 15:13 And he said unto Abram, Know of a surety that thy seed shall be a stranger in a land *that is* not theirs, and shall serve them; and they shall afflict them four hundred years;

Abraham is not the father of the entire WORLD, and of his seeds, it is specific with ONE seed.

Which Seed of Abraham Is Under the Covenant?
As you noticed, The Most High God told Abraham that thy SEED, which is referring to one man. If he had said SEEDS, then it would be all inclusive.

Genesis 17:17 Then Abraham fell upon his face, and laughed, and said in his heart, Shall *a child* be born unto him that is an hundred years old? and shall Sarah, that is ninety years old, bear?

Abraham LOVED The Most High God, but he was also human. He was one hundred years old, and Sarah was ninety. Childbearing years were behind them, he thought to himself, but The Most High heard him.

Genesis 17:18 And Abraham said unto God, O that Ishmael might live before thee!

Abraham tried to bring up Ishmael that The Most High will make a Covenant, because he thought that it was too late for Sarah and him to have a child.

The BLOOD of The Covenants

Genesis 17:19 And God said, Sarah thy wife shall bear thee a son indeed; and thou shalt call his name Isaac: and I will establish my covenant with him for an everlasting covenant, *and* with his seed after him.

The Most High rejected that thought, and told Abraham that Sarah will have a Son and you shall call him Isaac. The Most High said that He will make a Covenant with Isaac, not all his other seeds, including Ishmael, the children that he had by Keturah, and concubines.

Genesis 17:20 And as for Ishmael, I have heard thee: Behold, I have blessed him, and will make him fruitful, and will multiply him exceedingly; twelve princes shall he beget, and I will make him a great nation.

The Most High acknowledged Ismael, making him a prince, but The Most High God did not make a Covenant with Ishmael.

Genesis 15:14 And also that nation, whom they shall serve, will I judge: and afterward shall they come out with great substance.

The people who went into slavery in Egypt for over four hundred years and in America for over four hundred year will come out with great substance.

Isaiah 60:9 Surely the isles shall wait for me, and the ships of Tarshish first, to bring thy sons from far, their silver and their gold with them, unto the name of the LORD thy God, and to the Holy One of Israel, because he hath glorified thee.

The nations will deliver all of that gold and silver that they stole, returning it to The Most High God and Christ.

Genesis 15:15 And thou shalt go to thy fathers in peace; thou shalt be buried in a good old age.

I left this precept to show you that The Most High keeps His Covenants and promises even after you are dead and buried.

The BLOOD of The Covenants

Genesis 15:16 But in the fourth generation they shall come hither again: for the iniquity of the Amorites *is* not yet full.

The Most High told Abraham when his seed from Isaac will return.

Genesis 15:18 In the same day the LORD made a covenant with Abram, saying, Unto thy seed have I given this land, from the river of Egypt unto the great river, the river Euphrates:

This is the land between the Nile River and the River Euphrates, known as the Fertile Crescent. The Most High gave the Israelites the best portion of the land.

Deuteronomy 32:8 When the most High divided to the nations their inheritance, when he separated the sons of Adam, he set the bounds of the people according to the number of the children of Israel.

When The Most High God separated the Israelites from the nations, do you think He placed them in the deserts.

Deuteronomy 32:9 For the LORD'S portion *is* his people; Jacob *is* the lot of his inheritance.

Do you think that The Most High will give His inheritance a lesser portion of the land?

Genesis 15:19 The Kenites, and the Kenizzites, and the Kadmonites,

Genesis 15:20 And the Hittites, and the Perizzites, and the Rephaims,

Genesis 15:21 And the Amorites, and the Canaanites, and the Girgashites, and the Jebusites.

All these nations were destroyed for the Israelite's sake. This proves that The GOD of Abraham, Isaac and Jacob, is not the GOD of ALL NATIONS.

The BLOOD of The Covenants

What Does the GOD of Abraham, Isaac, and Jacob Think About the Nations?

This TRUTH must be known to ALL people. This is part of the KNOWLEDGE of the God of Abraham, Isaac, and Jacob.

Isaiah 40:15 Behold, the nations *are* as a drop of a bucket, and are counted as the small dust of the balance: behold, he taketh up the isles as a very little thing.

This is what The Most High thinks about ALL the NATIONS outside of the Israelites. Nobody considers a small drop of water that falls out of a full bucket of water, or a small speck of dust on a scale that has no weight. This is the CURSE for BREAKING His Covenant, because all these nations rule over us.

2 Esdras 6:57 And now, O Lord, behold, these heathen, which have ever been reputed as nothing, have begun to be lords over us, and to devour us.

Because the CHOSEN of GOD refuses to honor the Covenant that He made with their Fathers, then ALL these CURSES have overtaken the Israelites. Israelites are subjected to EVIL things wherever they live

2 Esdras 6:58 But we thy people, whom thou hast called thy firstborn, thy only begotten, and thy fervent lover, are given into their hands.

The Most High God, Our husband, has caught the Israelites CHEATING on Him with other gods many times, until He eventually kicked us out of His House, His presence, until we HUMBLE ourselves and are CONTRITE. Many Israelites who have gained some knowledge of the TRUTH are still too PROUD.

Psalms 138:6 Though the LORD *be* high, yet hath he respect unto the lowly: but the proud he knoweth afar off.

The Most High only RESPECT the HUMBLE and CONTRITE! When you are PROUD, you are not getting any blessings. Though He knows the PROUD, but they have not reached the plateau to receive any BENEFITS of the HUMBLE.

10

The BLOOD of The Covenants

2 Esdras 6:59 If the world now be made for our sakes, why do we not possess an inheritance with the world? how long shall this endure?

The answer to that question is that the Israelites are still too PROUD! They have committed many corruptible SINS, but they REFUSE to come to The Most High as He COMMANDS them. They come to Him like CAIN, the son of ADAM. Cain acknowledged The Most High God, but He did not have a humble and contrite spirit like his Brother, Abel.

Isaiah 40:16 And Lebanon *is* not sufficient to burn, nor the beasts thereof sufficient for a burnt offering.

The other nations can cut down all the trees in Lebanon and offer up all cattle, goats and sheep, but they still will be counted as a drop that falls out of a bucket.

Isaiah 40:17 All nations before him *are* as nothing; and they are counted to him less than nothing, and vanity.

The Most High God and Christ never moved from this position. Christ did not come to save the entire WORLD. That has never been the focus of this BIBLE

Matthew 18:11 For the Son of man is come to save that which was lost.

The Israelites are a people with an IDENTITY CRISIS! We do not know who we are. We only identify with names that the slave owners gave the people in the land. For example, the tribe of Gad and Reuben were given the name "Indian," and were called SAVAGES to justify destroying them and taking their inheritance. Native Americans, African American, Mexican, Puerto Rican, Haitian, etc., are all names given to The Most High God's people by their oppressors.

The BLOOD of The Covenants

Chapter 2: The Bloodline of the Covenant

Before I can get to the Covenants, I must continue with the Bloodline, because The Most High told Abraham that HIS SEED will inherit the kingdom. Right now, I am showing you WHICH SEED.

Genesis 25:21 And Isaac intreated the LORD for his wife, because she *was* barren: and the LORD was intreated of him, and Rebekah his wife conceived.

Isaac earnestly prayed for Rebekah to get pregnant, because she was not able to conceive. They had been trying for almost twenty years to conceive a child. The Most High heard Isaac and granted his request.

Genesis 25:22 And the children struggled together within her; and she said, If *it be* so, why *am* I thus? And she went to enquire of the LORD.

This is the point where I want to engage you. As you can see, there are twins, and The Most High only chose ONE seed. Rebekah went to PRAY to The Most High, to get an understanding of why she was in so much pain, seeing that her pregnancy was a blessing from The Most High.

Genesis 25:23 And the LORD said unto her, Two nations *are* in thy womb, and two manner of people shall be separated from thy bowels; and *the one* people shall be stronger than *the other* people; and the elder shall serve the younger.

She received an answer regarding the children inside of her womb. Two separate nations will come from the two children, one stronger than the other, and the child that came out first shall serve the other.

Genesis 25:24 And when her days to be delivered were fulfilled, behold, *there were* twins in her womb.

We established that there were twins

The BLOOD of The Covenants

Genesis 25:25 And the first came out red, all over like an hairy garment; and they called his name Esau.

One child came out RED and HAIRY and they called him Esau. This is the so-called White man today. They fit the description. They are RED and HAIRY when they are born.

Genesis 25:26 And after that came his brother out, and his hand took hold on Esau's heel; and his name was called Jacob: and Isaac *was* threescore years old when she bare them.

They did not mention anything regarding the color of Jacob, because he was the color of everyone else in the WORLD at that time. There is no recorded history of the so-called White man during this time.

Jacob Receives the Blessing From Isaac
It was customary that the OLDEST son received the blessing of the inheritance from their father, but The Most High chose Jacob before they could do any good or bad, before they were born.

Genesis 27:1 And it came to pass, that when Isaac was old, and his eyes were dim, so that he could not see, he called Esau his eldest son, and said unto him, My son: and he said unto him, Behold, *here am* I.

I surmise that it was The Most High God's plan that Isaac would be blind in his old aga, because if he were not, Esau would have the blessing of the Inheritance. The Most High God's word never go out VOID, what He told Rebekah still stands.

Isaiah 55:11 So shall my word be that goeth forth out of my mouth: it shall not return unto me void, but it shall accomplish that which I please, and it shall prosper *in the thing* whereto I sent it.

The Most High God's Word, what He told Rebekah, that He chose Jacob, the second son, will not go out VOID.

Genesis 27:2 And he said, Behold now, I am old, I know not the day of my death:

13

The BLOOD of The Covenants

Isaac realized that his time upon Earth was short.

Genesis 27:3 Now therefore take, I pray thee, thy weapons, thy quiver and thy bow, and go out to the field, and take me *some* venison;

Isaac wanted Esau to go out in the field and hunt some deer, which he loved, and his reason for loving Esau.

Genesis 25:27 And the boys grew: and Esau was a cunning hunter, a man of the field; and Jacob *was* a plain man, dwelling in tents.

Esau was a cunning hunter, the same as the so-called White man today. However, the sons of Jacob are city dwellers who do not care for the countryside.

Genesis 25:28 And Isaac loved Esau, because he did eat of *his* venison: but Rebekah loved Jacob.

Isaac loved Esau, because he loved venison, but Rebekah loved Jacob because of what The Most High God told her. This informs me that Rebekah never told Isaac what The Most High had told her. One of Esau's parents needed to be UNBIASED towards him.

Genesis 27:4 And make me savory meat, such as I love, and bring *it* to me, that I may eat; that my soul may bless thee before I die.

Isaac was planning on blessing Esau before he died, but this is not what The Most High God told Rebekah. However, did Rebekah just prayed about it and did nothing?

James 2:20 But wilt thou know, O vain man, that faith without works is dead?

Rebekah got busy. She had FAITH in what The Most High God had told her, and she was willing to stake her LIFE on it, but she got busy and did the work, to make certain Jacob received the BLESSINGS. I LOVE Rebekah!

The BLOOD of The Covenants

Genesis 27:5 And Rebekah heard when Isaac spake to Esau his son. And Esau went to the field to hunt *for* venison, *and* to bring *it.*

The Most High God placed Rebekah in this position to hear Isaac, and even gave her the plan

Proverbs 20:24 Man's goings *are* of the LORD; how can a man then understand his own way?

The Most High God placed Rebekah in the position to HEAR Isaac. She never revealed to Isaac what The Most High had told her. This is the reason she LOVED Jacob and Isaac loved Esau.

Genesis 27:6 And Rebekah spake unto Jacob her son, saying, Behold, I heard thy father speak unto Esau thy brother, saying,

Rebekah came to Jacob to tell him what she heard.

Genesis 27:7 Bring me venison, and make me savory meat, that I may eat, and bless thee before the LORD before my death.

Remember, The Most High said that "Faith without Works is DEAD." Rebekah went into action, doing works, to accomplish her goal, to get Jacob the blessings from Isaac, her husband, who had lost his sight. Apparently, Rebekah was an excellent cook, who could make goat meat taste like deer meat.

Genesis 27:8 Now therefore, my son, obey my voice according to that which I command thee.

She ask Jacob to do as she commands.

Genesis 27:9 Go now to the flock, and fetch me from thence two good kids of the goats; and I will make them savory meat for thy father, such as he loveth:

She told him to go among the flock and get her two good baby goats, and she will make them taste like venison that Isaac loves.

The BLOOD of The Covenants

Genesis 27:10 And thou shalt bring *it* to thy father, that he may eat, and that he may bless thee before his death.

Take the goat meat to your father that I (Rebekah) cooked and he will eat it and give you the blessing before he dies.

Jacob Recognized That He and His Brother, Esau Were Different

I can understand Jacob's concerns, because as dark and hairless as I am, I can understand trying to pass off as a so-called White man..

Genesis 27:11 And Jacob said to Rebekah his mother, Behold, Esau my brother *is* a hairy man, and I *am* a smooth man:

Jacob was concerned! Isaac may not have sight, but he definitely can distinguish the difference between Jacob and Esau. One is smooth, without hair, and the other is hairy. That is easy, touch him and he will know.

Genesis 27:12 My father peradventure will feel me, and I shall seem to him as a deceiver; and I shall bring a curse upon me, and not a blessing.

This is a valid concern for Jacob. Isaac will easily know the difference between the two of them, because of the hair.

Genesis 27:13 And his mother said unto him, Upon me *be* thy curse, my son: only obey my voice, and go fetch me *them*.

Rebekah had so much FAITH in what she believed what The Most High God told her, that she told him that the curses would be upon her.

Genesis 27:15 And Rebekah took goodly raiment of her eldest son Esau, which *were* with her in the house, and put them upon Jacob her younger son:

Isaac was not without smell. Isaac knew the difference Esau and Jacob. Esau smell like the woods, so Rebekah had to emulate that smell upon Jacob.

The BLOOD of The Covenants

Genesis 27:16 And she put the skins of the kids of the goats upon his hands, and upon the smooth of his neck:

Rebekah had to also emulate the texture, or hairiness of Esau. She placed goat hair on Jacob's hands and his necks to fool Isaac that he was touching a hairy person, and the only hairy person that he knew was Esau.

Genesis 27:26 And his father Isaac said unto him, Come near now, and kiss me, my son.

After Rebekah had prepared the goat meat, making it taste like deer meat, Jacob was ready to receive the blessings.

Genesis 27:27 And he came near, and kissed him: and he smelled the smell of his raiment, and blessed him, and said, See, the smell of my son *is* as the smell of a field which the LORD hath blessed:

Jacob came near to Isaac as Esau with the goat hair and Esau's garments that he was wearing. Isaac smelled Jacob and the hair, the smell of outdoors made Isaac believe that it was Esau.

Genesis 27:28 Therefore God give thee of the dew of heaven, and the fatness of the earth, and plenty of corn and wine:

Isaac blessed Jacob. Everywhere that Jacob lives, there will be abundant rain. Jacob lives nowhere else, even in captivity. If there is no abundant rain in the land, then there is a 100 percent chance that those are not the descendants of Jacob. The word of The Most High God of Abraham, Isaac, and Jacob does not go out VOID.

Genesis 27:29 Let people serve thee, and nations bow down to thee: be lord over thy brethren, and let thy mother's sons bow down to thee: cursed *be* every one that curseth thee, and blessed *be* he that blesseth thee.

Even as the sons of Jacob are CURSED, the other nations bow down to us. We bring FLAVOR to the ENTIRE world!

The BLOOD of The Covenants

Matthew 5:13 Ye are the salt of the earth: but if the salt have lost his savor, wherewith shall it be salted? it is thenceforth good for nothing, but to be cast out, and to be trodden under foot of men.

The Israelites provides FLAVOR to the ENTIRE world. Though they may deny it, but everything produced is a product of Israelite flavor. No fashion is successful unless it is approved by or made popular by Israelites.

Chapter 3: Jacob's Seeds

The Most High God chose Abraham and made a Covenant with him. The Most High chose Isaac, instead of Ishmael, and of Isaac's two sons, The Most High chose Jacob over Esau. The Most High only focused on these descendants throughout the Bible.

Where Did Jacob's Wives Come From?

Isaac, Jacob's father, gave Jacob instruction in regards to who to take as a wife. Isaac did not tell Jacob to go out and marry any woman. Thus, Isaac maintained that the SEED of Israel was pure

Genesis 28:1 And Isaac called Jacob, and blessed him, and charged him, and said unto him, Thou shalt not take a wife of the daughters of Canaan.

The Most High does not want His Chosen to marry the other nations. This was Law before the BLOOD Covenant between The Most High GOD of Abraham, Isaac, and Jacob and the Israelites.

Deuteronomy 7:3 Neither shalt thou make marriages with them; thy daughter thou shalt not give unto his son, nor his daughter shalt thou take unto thy son.

The Most High did not want the Israelites marrying outside of our tribe, even from the beginning.

Genesis 28:2 Arise, go to Padanaram, to the house of Bethuel thy mother's father; and take thee a wife from thence of the daughters of Laban thy mother's brother.

Laban was Rebekah's brother. Isaac told Jacob to go to Rebekah's brother and take a wife from one of his daughters, which would be Jacob's first cousin.

Genesis 27:42 And these words of Esau her elder son were told to Rebekah: and she sent and called Jacob her younger son, and said unto him, Behold, thy brother Esau, as touching thee, doth comfort himself, *purposing* to kill thee.

Esau was angry with Jacob when he pretended to be Esau, went to Isaac, who was blind, and took the blessing. Esau planned to kill Jacob after the death of Isaac. Rebekah got wind of it and she told Jacob that Esau was planning to kill him.

Genesis 27:43 Now therefore, my son, obey my voice; and arise, flee thou to Laban my brother to Haran;

Haran was Rebekah and Laban's father, who was also Abraham's brother.

Genesis 11:26 And Terah lived seventy years, and begat Abram, Nahor, and Haran.

This is to prove that first cousin is not considered close of kin, because if it did, our forefathers would have been in Sin.

Leviticus 18:6 None of you shall approach to any that is near of kin to him, to uncover *their* nakedness: I *am* the LORD.

According to the LAWS of the GOD of Abraham, Isaac, and Jacob, sons, daughters, mothers, fathers, brother-in-law, father-in-law, daughter-in-law, aunts, uncles, nephews and nieces are considered close of kin. First cousins are not. It is accepted among the elites, but not among the common folks, because it is how wealth and traditions are maintained..

The Beginning of the Nation: the Sons of Jacob are Born

Genesis 29:15 And Laban said unto Jacob, Because thou *art* my brother, shouldest thou therefore serve me for nought? tell me, what *shall* thy wages *be*?

Laban knew Jacob was related to him and he did not think it was right for Jacob to serve him unless he was working for something

The BLOOD of The Covenants

Genesis 29:<u>16</u> And Laban had two daughters: the name of the elder *was* Leah, and the name of the younger *was* Rachel.

Laban had two daughters, Leah, and Rachel.

Genesis 29:<u>17</u> Leah *was* tender eyed; but Rachel was beautiful and well favored.

Genesis 29:<u>18</u> And Jacob loved Rachel; and said, I will serve thee seven years for Rachel thy younger daughter.

Jacob loved Rachel. He offered to serve Laban seven years for Rachel.

Genesis 29:<u>19</u> And Laban said, *It is* better that I give her to thee, than that I should give her to another man: abide with me.

Laban agreed, telling him it would be better to give her to Jacob than to another man

Genesis 29:<u>20</u> And Jacob served seven years for Rachel; and they seemed unto him *but* a few days, for the love he had to her.

Jacob served Laban seven years for Rachel

Genesis 29:<u>21</u> And Jacob said unto Laban, Give *me* my wife, for my days are fulfilled, that I may go in unto her.

Jacob asked Laban for Rachel after the seventh year of service.

Genesis 29:<u>22</u> And Laban gathered together all the men of the place, and made a feast.

This is a slick move by Laban for what he was about to do to Jacob. If Jacob got angry and violent then he would have some help subduing him.

Genesis 29:<u>23</u> And it came to pass in the evening, that he took Leah his daughter, and brought her to him; and he went in unto her.

The BLOOD of The Covenants

At sunset, Laban sneaked Leah into Jacob's room, and Jacob, thinking that it was Rachel, had sex with her to consummate the marriage

Genesis 29:24 And Laban gave unto his daughter Leah Zilpah his maid *for* an handmaid.

Laban gave Leah Zilpah for a handmaid.

Genesis 29:25 And it came to pass, that in the morning, behold, it *was* Leah: and he said to Laban, What *is* this thou hast done unto me? did not I serve with thee for Rachel? wherefore then hast thou beguiled me?

Jacob did not find out that it was Leah until the morning. Now, I am sure that Jacob was angry! He was deceived, thinking he was serving seven years for Rachel, but he got Leah. I am not saying that Leah was a bad choice, but she was not his initial goal.

Genesis 29:26 And Laban said, It must not be so done in our country, to give the younger before the firstborn.

Why did Laban not tell Jacob this in the beginning? Laban pulled one over on Jacob.

Genesis 29:27 Fulfil her week, and we will give thee this also for the service which thou shalt serve with me yet seven other years.

Laban said to give Leah her week and he will also give Jacob Rachel, but he will have to fulfill seven more years.

Genesis 29:28 And Jacob did so, and fulfilled her week: and he gave him Rachel his daughter to wife also.

Jacob had to serve Laban 14 years for Rachel. This looks nothing like the original agreement. It could be said that Laban was doing everything in his power to keep Jacob in his house.

The BLOOD of The Covenants

Genesis 30:<u>27</u> And Laban said unto him, I pray thee, if I have found favor in thine eyes, *tarry: for* I have learned by experience that the LORD hath blessed me for thy sake.

Laban knew The Most High was blessing his house because Jacob was dwelling with him.

Genesis 29:<u>29</u> And Laban gave to Rachel his daughter Bilhah his handmaid to be her maid.

Laban gave Rachel Bilhah as a handmaid.

Genesis 29:<u>30</u> And he went in also unto Rachel, and he loved also Rachel more than Leah, and served with him yet seven other years.

Jacob went into Rachel, consummating the marriage. Also, Jacob had to work for Laban seven more years.

Genesis 29:<u>31</u> And when the LORD saw that Leah *was* hated, he opened her womb: but Rachel *was* barren.

Jacob was spending more time with Rachel than with Leah. The Most High blessed Leah's womb.

Son #1 Reuben - Leah

Genesis 29:<u>32</u> And Leah conceived, and bare a son, and she called his name Reuben: for she said, Surely the LORD hath looked upon my affliction; now therefore my husband will love me.

Reuben – The LORD had seen my affliction.

Genesis 29:<u>33</u> And she conceived again, and bare a son; and said, Because the LORD hath heard that I *was* hated, he hath therefore given me this *son* also: and she called his name Simeon.

Son #2 Simeon – Leah

Leah bare Simeon – The LORD had heard that I was hated

The BLOOD of The Covenants

Genesis 29:<u>34</u> And she conceived again, and bare a son; and said, Now this time will my husband be joined unto me, because I have born him three sons: therefore was his name called Levi.

Son #3 Levi – Leah

Levi – Joined: Leah believed that Jacob will be "joined" unto her because she bares him three sons

Genesis 29:<u>35</u> And she conceived again, and bare a son: and she said, Now will I praise the LORD: therefore she called his name Judah; and left bearing.

Son #4 Judah – Leah
Judah - Meaning "Praise" or God's Praise

Genesis 30:<u>1</u> And when Rachel saw that she bare Jacob no children, Rachel envied her sister; and said unto Jacob, Give me children, or else I die.

Leah had four sons by Jacob, and Rachel had no children. She was jealous, panicking, demanding Jacob give her a child.

Genesis 30:<u>2</u> And Jacob's anger was kindled against Rachel: and he said, *Am* I in God's stead, who hath withheld from thee the fruit of the womb?

Jacob was angry with Rachel, with her thinking that he has control whether he can make her pregnant whenever he wanted.

Genesis 30:<u>3</u> And she said, Behold my maid Bilhah, go in unto her; and she shall bear upon my knees, that I may also have children by her.

Rachel gave Jacob Bilhah, her handmaid to conceive a child in her place

Genesis 30:<u>4</u> And she gave him Bilhah her handmaid to wife: and Jacob went in unto her.

Jacob married Bilhah and had sex with her.

Genesis 30:5 And Bilhah conceived, and bare Jacob a son.

Bilhah conceived and had a son.

Son #5 Dan – Bilhah, Rachel's handmaid

Genesis 30:6 And Rachel said, God hath judged me, and hath also heard my voice, and hath given me a son: therefore called she his name Dan.

Dan – God had Judged

Genesis 30:7 And Bilhah Rachel's maid conceived again, and bare Jacob a second son.

Son #6 Naphtali – Bilhah, Rachel's handmaid

Genesis 30:8 And Rachel said, With great wrestlings have I wrestled with my sister, and I have prevailed: and she called his name Naphtali.

Naphtali – "Struggled" and have prevailed

Genesis 30:9 When Leah saw that she had left bearing, she took Zilpah her maid, and gave her Jacob to wife.

Leah gave her handmaid, Zilpah to Jacob to wife

Genesis 30:10 And Zilpah Leah's maid bare Jacob a son.

Son #7 Gad – Zilpah, Leah's handmaid

Genesis 30:11 And Leah said, A troop cometh: and she called his name Gad.

Gad – a troop cometh

Genesis 30:12 And Zilpah Leah's maid bare Jacob a second son.

The BLOOD of The Covenants

Son #8 Asher – Zilpah, Leah's handmaid

Genesis 30:13 And Leah said, Happy am I, for the daughters will call me blessed: and she called his name Asher.

Asher – Happy or Blessed

Genesis 30:16 And Jacob came out of the field in the evening, and Leah went out to meet him, and said, Thou must come in unto me; for surely I have hired thee with my son's mandrakes. And he lay with her that night.

Leah gave Rachel some Mandrakes in order to sleep with Jacob, meaning Jacob likely stayed with Rachel as he loved her

Son #9 Issachar - Leah

Genesis 30:17 And God hearkened unto Leah, and she conceived, and bare Jacob the fifth son.

Genesis 30:18 And Leah said, God hath given me my hire, because I have given my maiden to my husband: and she called his name Issachar.

Issachar – Hire, wage, reward

Genesis 30:19 And Leah conceived again, and bare Jacob the sixth son.

Son #10 Zebulun - Leah

Genesis 30:20 And Leah said, God hath endued me *with* a good dowry; now will my husband dwell with me, because I have born him six sons: and she called his name Zebulun.

Zebulun – dowry, or to dwell

Genesis 30:22 And God remembered Rachel, and God hearkened to her, and opened her womb.

The BLOOD of The Covenants

Son #11 Joseph - Rachel

Genesis 30:23 And she conceived, and bare a son; and said, God hath taken away my reproach:

Genesis 30:24 And she called his name Joseph; and said, The LORD shall add to me another son.

Joseph – The Most High Shall Add

Genesis 30:25 And it came to pass, when Rachel had born Joseph, that Jacob said unto Laban, Send me away, that I may go unto mine own place, and to my country.

Son #12 Benjamin – Rachel

Genesis 35:16 And they journeyed from Bethel; and there was but a little way to come to Ephrath: and Rachel travailed, and she had hard labor.

Rachel final pregnancy was exceedingly difficult

Genesis 35:17 And it came to pass, when she was in hard labor, that the midwife said unto her, Fear not; thou shalt have this son also.

Genesis 35:18 And it came to pass, as her soul was in departing, (for she died) that she called his name Benoni: but his father called him Benjamin.

Benjamin – son of the right (Source: https://www.ancient-hebrew.org/names/Benjamin.htm

Chapter 4: The Children of Jacob Must Serve 400 Years

As The Most High God told Abraham, that his seed will serve hard bondage for four hundred years. The children of Ishmael, Esau, the sons of Keturah, none of them went into captivity.

Genesis 46:2 And God spake unto Israel in the visions of the night, and said, Jacob, Jacob. And he said, Here *am* I.

The Most High God called Jacob in a VISION at night.

Genesis 46:3 And he said, I *am* God, the God of thy father: fear not to go down into Egypt; for I will there make of thee a great nation:

The Most High God told Jacob who He was, that He IS the God of HIS FATHERS, not the GOD of EVERYBODY. He told Jacob to go into Egypt, because this is part of the plan.

Genesis 46:4 I will go down with thee into Egypt; and I will also surely bring thee up *again*: and Joseph shall put his hand upon thine eyes.

The Most High went into Egypt with His servant, Jacob, and He will bring the Israelites up, and Joseph will put his hand upon his eyes.

Genesis 46:5 And Jacob rose up from Beersheba: and the sons of Israel carried Jacob their father, and their little ones, and their wives, in the wagons which Pharaoh had sent to carry him.

This is FAITH. When The Most High told Jacob to go into Egypt, you see his response? HE PACKED THEM ALL UP in the wagons

Genesis 46:6 And they took their cattle, and their goods, which they had gotten in the land of Canaan, and came into Egypt, Jacob, and all his seed with him:

The BLOOD of The Covenants

Jacob brought all of his seed, including his sons and all of their children.

Genesis 46:7 His sons, and his sons' sons with him, his daughters, and his sons' daughters, and all his seed brought he with him into Egypt.

Apparently Jacob had daughters, which means that he had a daughter other than Dinah.

Genesis 46:26 All the souls that came with Jacob into Egypt, which came out of his loins, besides Jacob's sons' wives, all the souls *were* threescore and six;

All the people that rolled into Egypt, an already GREAT NATION, was sixty-six people

Genesis 46:27 And the sons of Joseph, which were born him in Egypt, *were* two souls: all the souls of the house of Jacob, which came into Egypt, *were* threescore and ten.

When you add Joseph, his Egyptian wife, Ephraim, and Manasseh, that number increased to seventy. Yes, Joseph's wife was counted because Joseph was a servant in the land, and The Most High do not ever want us to be alone.

The BLOOD of The Covenants

The Most High God Made Certain That Israel Remain Separate

The Egyptians though lowly of shepherds, so they were permitted to live in Goshen.

Genesis 47:3 And Pharaoh said unto his brethren, What *is* your occupation? And they said unto Pharaoh, Thy servants *are* shepherds, both we, *and* also our fathers.

Pharaoh asked the sons of Jacob what their Job skill was?. They told him that they were shepherds, and so was their father.

Genesis 47:4 They said moreover unto Pharaoh, For to sojourn in the land are we come; for thy servants have no pasture for their flocks; for the famine *is* sore in the land of Canaan: now therefore, we pray thee, let thy servants dwell in the land of Goshen.

The sons of Jacob requested the land of Goshen, because Joseph told them to request this land.

Genesis 47:5 And Pharaoh spake unto Joseph, saying, Thy father and thy brethren are come unto thee:

Genesis 47:6 The land of Egypt *is* before thee; in the best of the land make thy father and brethren to dwell; in the land of Goshen let them dwell: and if thou knowest *any* men of activity among them, then make them rulers over my cattle.

This is all plan of The Most High God, that Israel, as a young nation, remain separated from the Hamites.

The Nation of Israel Grew In Egypt and Were Placed Into Slavery

This seems to be our CURSE: when the other nations cannot BENEFIT from you, they have no need for the men, place us into slavery, and kill our children. Is this happening today?

Exodus 1:6 And Joseph died, and all his brethren, and all that generation.

The BLOOD of The Covenants

All the sons of Jacob were now gone

Exodus 1:7 And the children of Israel were fruitful, and increased abundantly, and multiplied, and waxed exceeding mighty; and the land was filled with them.

The descendants of Jacob, or Israel, let me get you familiar with Israel.

Genesis 32:28 And he said, Thy name shall be called no more Jacob, but Israel: for as a prince hast thou power with God and with men, and hast prevailed.

Jacob's name was changed to ISRAEL by The Most High God. Israel has meaning to The Most High, African American, Mexican, Jamaican, Haitian, Dominican, Puerto Rican, Panamanian, Ghanian, Congolese, Senegalese, etc., do not have value to The Most High. These names were given to us by those who conquered us.

Exodus 1:8 Now there arose up a new king over Egypt, which knew not Joseph.

After Joseph died, the new king of Egypt did not know, or did not want to know what Joseph did to save their people. I will say that the new king did not care.

Exodus 1:9 And he said unto his people, Behold, the people of the children of Israel *are* more and mightier than we:

This is the EXCUSE to justify his actions of placing the children of Israel into slavery. Imagine, we came into Egypt, only sixty-six people, seventy total with Joseph and his family. Now, Israel outnumbers the Egyptians. Israel has always been fruitful.

Exodus 1:10 Come on, let us deal wisely with them; lest they multiply, and it come to pass, that, when there falleth out any war, they join also unto our enemies, and fight against us, and *so* get them up out of the land.

The BLOOD of The Covenants

This king was simply justifying the actions that he was about to take. If he was concerned because of our numbers, why not create a relationship with us?

Exodus 1:11 Therefore they did set over them taskmasters to afflict them with their burdens. And they built for Pharaoh treasure cities, Pithom and Rameses.

The first thing they did was organize and made some of the Israelite men taskmasters, to afflict us with something similar to the 13th Amendment, making us SLAVES. In order to understand, the Israelites were skilled in all sorts of crafts. We built the Pyramids!

Exodus 1:12 But the more they afflicted them, the more they multiplied and grew. And they were grieved because of the children of Israel.

Just because the Israelites were afflicted did not translate into us not having sex and children. We still multiplied as The Most High God instructed.

Genesis 1:28 And God blessed them, and God said unto them, Be fruitful, and multiply, and replenish the earth, and subdue it: and have dominion over the fish of the sea, and over the fowl of the air, and over every living thing that moveth upon the earth.

Regardless of our situation today, the Israelites will still have sex and have children, even though it is not according to how society has been established.

Exodus 1:13 And the Egyptians made the children of Israel to serve with rigor:

The Egyptians placed us into hard bondage! Do you that the Israelites were not praying for help? Do you think that they were praying for the WHOLE WORLD, who were not in hard bondage?

The BLOOD of The Covenants

Exodus 1:15 And the king of Egypt spake to the Hebrew midwives, of which the name of the one *was* Shiphrah, and the name of the other Puah:

A **MIDWIFE** is a woman trained to assist women in childbirth. Shiphrah and Puah were women trained in childbirth.

Exodus 1:16 And he said, When ye do the office of a midwife to the Hebrew women, and see *them* upon the stools; if it *be* a son, then ye shall kill him: but if it *be* a daughter, then she shall live.

The Pharaoh instructed Shiphrah and Puah to only deliver the females and KILL all the male Israelite babies, because he knew the seed is from the man, and they did not want any more male Israelite babies born in Egypt.

Exodus 1:17 But the midwives feared God, and did not as the king of Egypt commanded them, but saved the men children alive.

The women today, who are ABORTING their babies, do not FEAR THEIR GOD. They do not UNDERSTAND what they are supposed to be doing in the first place.

Psalms 111:10 The fear of the LORD *is* the beginning of wisdom: a good understanding have all they that do *his commandments*: his praise endureth forever.

The Israelite women today, do not FEAR their GOD . They do not know him. Abortion is free and available, and they have CHOICE to choose. They do not need a Hebrew man, nor do they need His LAWS to GUIDE them.

The BLOOD of The Covenants

Chapter 5: The Most High God Uses Moses to Free His People As He Promised Abraham.

The Most High God promised Abraham that his seed would serve bondage for four hundred years, and He will deliver them.

Exodus 3:1 Now Moses kept the flock of Jethro his father in law, the priest of Midian: and he led the flock to the backside of the desert, and came to the mountain of God, *even* to Horeb.

The Mountain of The Most High God is Mount Sinai, or Mount Horeb. (**source: https://bibleatlas.org/mount_horeb.htm**). Moses was living with an Ethiopian Druid Priest, and I am certain that he was involved, somewhat, in that religion.

Let us understand what a Midian Priest was

Jethro - Moses' father-in-law is initially referred to as "Reuel" (Exodus 2:18) but then as "Jethro" (Exodus 3:1). He was the father of Hobab in the Book of Numbers 10:29.[2] He is also revered as the spiritual founder and chief prophet in his own right of the Druze religion[3][4][5] and is considered an ancestor of all Druze.

Source: https://en.wikipedia.org/wiki/Jethro_(biblical_figure)

Druze Religion - The **Druze** beliefs incorporate elements of Ismailism, Gnosticism, Neoplatonism and other philosophies. The **Druze** call themselves Ahl al-Tawhid "People of Unitarianism or Monotheism" or "al-Muwaḥḥidūn." "The **Druze** follow a lifestyle of isolation where no conversion is allowed, neither out of, or into, the **religion**.

Source: https://en.wikipedia.org/wiki/Lebanese_Druze

Moses' Father-in-law was not a Hebrew Priest serving the GOD of Abraham, Isaac, and Jacob. Jethro was also a Hamite, an Ethiopian, and Moses' wife was also of that nation. Did The Most High punish Moses for marrying an Ethiopian woman?

The BLOOD of The Covenants

Exodus 3:2 And the angel of the LORD appeared unto him in a flame of fire out of the midst of a bush: and he looked, and, behold, the bush burned with fire, and the bush *was* not consumed.

The Angel of The Most High appeared unto Moses in a FLAME. This shows that, regardless of your circumstances, if you are of the Elect, The Most High reveals Himself to whom He pleases.

Exodus 3:3 And Moses said, I will now turn aside, and see this great sight, why the bush is not burnt.

Moses was CURIOUS, so He turned to see why the bush was on fire, but not burning.

Exodus 3:4 And when the LORD saw that he turned aside to see, God called unto him out of the midst of the bush, and said, Moses, Moses. And he said, Here *am* I.

Moses answered the LORD, as planned

Isaiah 46:10 Declaring the end from the beginning, and from ancient times *the things* that are not *yet* done, saying, My counsel shall stand, and I will do all my pleasure:

The Most High knew Moses would be curious, and He knew that Moses would answer.

Exodus 3:5 And he said, Draw not nigh hither: put off thy shoes from off thy feet, for the place whereon thou standest *is* holy ground.

Did The Most High really mean for Moses to take off his shoes, or did He mean something else entirely?

What did The LORD mean by this?

Ecclesiastes 5:1 Keep thy foot when thou goest to the house of God, and be more ready to hear, than to give the sacrifice of fools: for they consider not that they do evil.

The BLOOD of The Covenants

The Angel of The Most High God was basically telling Moses to not give Him the Druze Religion that he learned from Jethro, his father-in-law, be more ready to LISTEN, than sound like a FOOL.

Exodus 3:6 Moreover he said, I *am* the God of thy father, the God of Abraham, the God of Isaac, and the God of Jacob. And Moses hid his face; for he was afraid to look upon God.

The GOD whom I worship is the same GOD who introduced Himself to Moses, The God of Abraham, Isaac, and Jacob. When Moses knew who He was speaking, he became afraid.

Exodus 3:7 And the LORD said, I have surely seen the affliction of my people which *are* in Egypt, and have heard their cry by reason of their taskmasters; for I know their sorrows;

The Most High could have gone and destroyed Egypt, but the other nations would not have known why The Most High destroyed them, or whose behalf they were destroyed. He promised Abraham that He would bring them out on his behalf.

Exodus 3:8 And I am come down to deliver them out of the hand of the Egyptians, and to bring them up out of that land unto a good land and a large, unto a land flowing with milk and honey; unto the place of the Canaanites, and the Hittites, and the Amorites, and the Perizzites, and the Hivites, and the Jebusites.

The Most High needed a FAITHFUL Hebrew to represent Him, and not question His every decision. The land that The Most High showed Abraham was between the Egypt river and the Euphrates River.

Exodus 3:9 Now therefore, behold, the cry of the children of Israel is come unto me: and I have also seen the oppression wherewith the Egyptians oppress them.

The captivity that the Israelites were held under the Egyptians was a very harsh captivity, similar to the captivity that we are held under today

The BLOOD of The Covenants

Exodus 3:10 Come now therefore, and I will send thee unto Pharaoh, that thou mayest bring forth my people the children of Israel out of Egypt.

Chapter 6: A Brief Explanation of The Exodus

As The Most High God made a Covenant with Abraham, and promised him, He will deliver on His Promise. This is a short synopsis of what transpired in Egypt.

Psalms 105:26 He sent Moses his servant; *and* Aaron whom he had chosen.

Moses was an outsider, who was raised in the Pharaoh's home, but rejected it, He was nurtured by his mother.

Moses Gained History of His Family, Miriam and Aaron Because His Mother Nurtured Him.
We must understand that Moses was FOSTERED as a child, then how did He get knowledge of his family?

Exodus 2:3 And when she could not longer hide him, she took for him an ark of bulrushes, and daubed it with slime and with pitch, and put the child therein; and she laid *it* in the flags by the river's brink.

There was a Law imposed by the Pharaoh to kill all Israelite male babies. Moses's mother could no longer hide him, so she built a small little floating vessel, placed Moses in it, and had Miriam watch what happened to it.

Exodus 2:4 And his sister stood afar off, to wit what would be done to him.

That Sister is Miriam. She watched her baby brother to see what would happen to him.

Exodus 2:5 And the daughter of Pharaoh came down to wash *herself* at the river; and her maidens walked along by the river's side; and when she saw the ark among the flags, she sent her maid to fetch it.

Pharaoh's daughter sent her maiden to retrieve baby Moses from the water

The BLOOD of The Covenants

Exodus 2:6 And when she had opened *it*, she saw the child: and, behold, the babe wept. And she had compassion on him, and said, This *is one* of the Hebrews' children.

When she saw how handsome Moses was, and he began crying, Pharaoh's daughter was compassionate to him.

Exodus 2:7 Then said his sister to Pharaoh's daughter, Shall I go and call to thee a nurse of the Hebrew women, that she may nurse the child for thee?

Miriam, Moses's sister, asked Pharaoh's daughter, "do you want me to go find among the Hebrew women to nurse him?"

Exodus 2:8 And Pharaoh's daughter said to her, Go. And the maid went and called the child's mother.

Moses's mother was re-introduced back into Moses life

Exodus 2:9 And Pharaoh's daughter said unto her, Take this child away, and nurse it for me, and I will give *thee* thy wages. And the woman took the child, and nursed it.

Moses's mother was employed as his nurse, and Moses knew Miriam and Moses, because the mother brought them around him.

Psalms 105:27 They shewed his signs among them, and wonders in the land of Ham.

Moses and Aaron showed signs and wonders in Egypt, the descendants of Ham.

Psalms 105:28 He sent darkness, and made it dark; and they rebelled not against his word.

When The Most High sent all of this DARKNESS, and the Israelites did not REBEL against His Law. This is not how it is today. The Israelites are in DARKNESS and are REBELLIOUS!

The BLOOD of The Covenants

Psalms 105:29 He turned their waters into blood, and slew their fish.

This is the DARKNESS that The Most High God sent upon the land.

Psalms 105:30 Their land brought forth frogs in abundance, in the chambers of their kings.

The Most High sent pestilence of frogs, even in the chambers of the kings.

Psalms 105:31 He spake, and there came divers sorts of flies, *and* lice in all their coasts.

Another DARKNESS is when The Most High God sent diverse flies, lice.

Psalms 105:32 He gave them hail for rain, *and* flaming fire in their land.

When The Most High was sending all of this DARKNESS, the Israelites were in FEAR.

Psalms 105:33 He smote their vines also and their fig trees; and brake the trees of their coasts.

Psalms 105:34 He spake, and the locusts came, and caterpillars, and that without number,

The Most High sent another DARKNESS in the abundance of locust and caterpillars.

Psalms 105:35 And did eat up all the herbs in their land, and devoured the fruit of their ground.

Imagine how catastrophic locust and caterpillars are to crops and farms. The powers that exist today seem to be creating a catastrophic failure of food. They began with the slowing down the supply chain, letting freight just sit at docks without being released for pickup. The USA USDA have threatened many farmers that they will stop paying them, if they did not destroy their crops. They were paid one and a half time more to destroy their crops than to plant them. They would also get more money, based upon how they destroyed their crops: whether they dug them up or use pesticides.

Psalms 105:36 He smote also all the firstborn in their land, the chief of all their strength.

The Passover

Exodus 12:1 And the LORD spake unto Moses and Aaron in the land of Egypt, saying,

The Most High spoke to Moses and Aaron while we were still in Egypt.

Exodus 12:2 This month shall be unto you the beginning of months: it shall be the first month of the year to you.

The Month of Abib is the FIRST MONTH to the Israelites

The Month of Abib, the New Moon in March, is the FIRST MONTH to the Israelites

Exodus 13:4 This day came ye out in the month Abib.

Abib - the first month of the ancient Hebrew calendar corresponding to Nisan

Hebrew *Ābhībh*, literally, ear of grain

The Month of Abib is the New Year for Those Who The Most High Delivered Out of Egypt.

This is not the same New Year as January 1, for the other nations. The people that The Most High delivered out of Egypt, their New Year begins in the Spring, the first New Moon in March.

What Were the Israelites Instructed to Do?

These instructions were given to the Israelites, a people who were in captivity in Egypt, not to the ENTIRE world

The BLOOD of The Covenants

Exodus 12:3_Speak ye unto all the congregation of Israel, saying, In the tenth <u>day</u> of this month they shall take to them every man a lamb, according to the house of <u>their</u> fathers, a lamb for an house:

The Congregation of Israel were the people in captivity, who built road, planted crops, raised cattle, raised the Egyptian children, built Pyramids, etc. The tenth day of this month, every man of a family is ordered to get a lamb for his house. Let us understand, first, how to determine the New Year.

How Do We Determine the Israelite New Year?
I always will provide this information, so that we can determine The Most High God's Holy Days. You must be DILIGENT in DETERMINING When to OBSERVE The Most High God's Holy Days.

Deuteronomy 28:1_And it shall come to pass, if thou shalt hearken **diligently** unto the voice of the LORD thy God, to **observe** *and* to do **ALL** his commandments which I command thee this day, that the LORD thy God will set thee on high above all nations of the earth:

This is where many Hebrews find themselves lacking. They are not **DILIGENT,** and are following the doctrine of men.

How Do We Determine The Most High God's Feast Days?
Ecclesiasticus 43:6_He made the moon also to serve in her season for a declaration of times, and a sign of the world.

The Most High created the MOON to let the Israelites know the time of season, the time of month and the time of year. The MOON declares the New Year. Which Moon is the New Moon? Is it that DARK MOON?

Ecclesiasticus 43:7_From the moon is the sign of feasts, a light that decreaseth in her perfection.

The Israelites DETERMINE the FEASTS from the MOON THAT DECREASES IN ITS PERFECT SIZE. This is the FULL MOON.

The FULL MOON is also the NEW MOON (a moon that decreases in its perfection). On the tenth day of the New Year, which is ten days after the FULL MOON, each Israelite family should have their lamb secured during this time.

If You Are Not Diligent, You Will Be Worshiping The Most High God On A Regular Day, Not A Distinguished Day.

Ecclesiasticus 33:7 Why doth one day excel another, when as all the light of every day in the year is of the sun?

The question asked is why is one day greater than another when every day, the Sun shines upon them equally? This tells you that every day is NOT the same, even though the sun shines on them equally.

Ecclesiasticus 33:8 By the knowledge of the Lord they were distinguished: and he altered seasons and feasts.

The Most High God DISTINGUISHED the Holy Days through His knowledge, which He gave to the Israelites through His Laws, Statues and Commandments. If you do not determine the correct NEW MOON, then you are worshiping The Most High on an ORDINARY DAY, the same as those worshiping Him on Sunday.

Ecclesiasticus 33:9 Some of them hath he made high days, and hallowed them, and some of them hath he made ordinary days.

You must be DILIGENT in the Law, even when you are determining the HIGH HOLY DAYS, which are set apart by The Most High God. The Most High Distinguished Holy Days, like the Sabbath, New Moons, Passover, etc.

Ezekiel 22:26 Her priests have violated my law, and have profaned mine holy things: they have put no difference between the holy and profane, neither have they shewed *difference* between the unclean and the clean, and have hid their eyes from my sabbaths, and I am profaned among them.

Through our LEADERSHIP, in the Hebrew Community, Christianity, Islam, Egyptology, Politics, etc. They are profaning The Most High God's people. They hide our people from The Most High God's Holy

The BLOOD of The Covenants

Days, including the Sabbath, New Moons and Passover. Even those in the Hebrew Community are hiding themselves from The Most High God's Feast days, which you are supposed to treat like Sabbaths.

Exodus 12:4 And if the household be too little for the lamb, let him and his neighbor next unto his house take it according to the number of the souls; every man according to his eating shall make your count for the lamb.

Concerning this lamb for the Passover, you do not have to buy a whole lamb if your family is too small to eat it. You can split it with your neighbor who also has a small family. This was specific to the nation of Israel when we were together as a nation. Now, we are separated among our enemies.

Exodus 12:5 Your lamb shall be without blemish, a male of the first year: ye shall take it out from the sheep, or from the goats:

It must be a MALE lamb without blemish, or a male goat without blemish.

Exodus 12:6 And ye shall keep it up until the fourteenth day of the same month: and the whole assembly of the congregation of Israel shall kill it in the evening.

Keep the lamb until the fourteenth day, which is the Passover. The entire congregation shall kill the lamb in the evening, at sunset.

Exodus 12:7 And they shall take of the blood, and strike it on the two side posts and on the upper door post of the houses, wherein they shall eat it.

The congregation took the blood and slapped it on the two-sided post and on the upper door, in the house where the lamb will be eaten. This is what the Israelites were instructed to do during the actual Passover, when they were held captive in Egypt.

Exodus 12:8 And they shall eat the flesh in that night, roast with fire, and unleavened bread; and with bitter herbs they shall eat it.

The BLOOD of The Covenants

The lamb MUST be roasted with fire, not broiled, boiled. You also must have UNLEAVENED BREAD, bread cooked without a rising agent, such as yeast, baking powder or baking soda, and it must be eaten with bitter herbs.

Exodus 12:9 Eat not of it raw, nor sodden at all with water, but roast with fire; his head with his legs, and with the purtenance thereof.

Purtenance - An animal's viscera or internal organs, especially the heart, liver, and lungs.

We are instructed to cook the entire lamb, including his head, legs and his internal organs. We are commanded to not eat it raw or boiled.

Exodus 12:10 And ye shall let nothing of it remain until the morning; and that which remaineth of it until the morning ye shall burn with fire.

During the Passover, all lamb MUST be eaten before morning. Anything that is leftover MUST be burned with fire.

Exodus 12:11 And thus shall ye eat it; with your loins girded, your shoes on your feet, and your staff in your hand; and ye shall eat it in haste: it is the LORD'S Passover.

Gird Up Your Loins
Source: https://www.artofmanliness.com/articles/how-to-gird-up-your-loins-an-illustrated-guide/

Back in the days of the ancient Near East, both men and women wore flowing tunics. Around the tunic, they would wear a belt or girdle. While tunics were comfortable and breezy, the hem of the tunic would often get in the way when a man was fighting or performing hard labor. So, when ancient Hebrew men had to battle the Philistines, the men would lift the hem of their tunic up and tuck it into their girdle or tie it in a knot to keep it off the ground. The effect basically created a pair of shorts that provided more freedom of movement. Thus, to tell someone to "gird up their loins" was to tell them to get ready for challenging work or battle. It was the ancient way of saying "man up!"

The BLOOD of The Covenants

The Hebrew men are commanded to eat the Passover meal with their Loins Girded, shoes on their feet and staff in their hand, and they shall eat it quickly.

Exodus 12:12 For I will pass through the land of Egypt this night, and will smite all the firstborn in the land of Egypt, both man and beast; and against all the gods of Egypt I will execute judgment: I am the LORD.

The Most High, Himself, did not pass through the land, but "EVIL ANGELS" did.

Psalms 78:49 He cast upon them the fierceness of his anger, wrath, and indignation, and trouble, by sending evil angels *among them.*

The Most High God is the HEAD. He COMMANDS and sends Christ and His Angels to do His WILL. It is not in them to question His COMMANDMENTS. The Most High sent them to destroy the Egyptians on our behalf.

Psalms 78:50 He made a way to his anger; he spared not their soul from death, but gave their life over to the pestilence.

The Most High did not spare the Egyptians from death.

Psalms 78:51 And smote all the firstborn in Egypt; the chief of *their* strength in the tabernacles of Ham:

The Egyptians are descendants of Ham, so are the Babylonians!

Exodus 12:13 And the blood shall be to you for a token upon the houses where ye are: and when I see the blood, I will pass over you, and the plague shall not be upon you to destroy you, when I smite the land of Egypt.

Those Evil Angels that The Most High God sent shall see the BLOOD on the two post and above the door and will PASS OVER that house. Can the CORONAVIRUS be another Evil Angel that will PASS OVER the Saints who are keeping the Commandments?

The BLOOD of The Covenants

Exodus 12:14 And this day shall be unto you for a memorial; and ye shall keep it a feast to the LORD throughout your generations; ye shall keep it a feast by an ordinance forever.

Memorial - something, especially a structure, established to remind people of a person or event.
The Passover shall be a MEMORIAL and the ISRAELITES shall keep it as a FEAST to The Most High FOREVER. It is a LAW, only for the Israelites.

Exodus 12:15 Seven days shall ye eat unleavened bread; even the first day ye shall put away leaven out of your houses: for whosoever eateth leavened bread from the first day until the seventh day, that soul shall be cut off from Israel.

The Passover Feast shall last seven days, in which the Israelites are COMMANDED to eat UNLEAVENED BREAD. The First day, all rising agents shall be removed from your home.

Exodus 12:16 And in the first day there shall be an holy convocation, and in the seventh day there shall be an holy convocation to you; no manner of work shall be done in them, save that which every man must eat, that only may be done of you.

The first day and the last day shall be a holy gathering. We shall do no work. We know that we are in captivity today. Some of us have jobs that require us to work on these days.

Philippians 2:12 Wherefore, my beloved, as ye have always obeyed, not as in my presence only, but now much more in my absence, work out your own salvation with fear and trembling.

If you must work, it does not mean that you must buy anything. When you get off work, put your fringed garments on. If you are able to gather with your RIGHTEOUS Brothers and Sisters, then gather with them. If you are not able, find a Hebrew gathering online and congregate with them. Make an effort.

The BLOOD of The Covenants

Chapter 7: The Laws Before the Covenant

This is The Most High showing His Word to Jacob, His Statues and Judgments to Israel

Exodus 20:1 And God spake all these words, saying,

All of the following words were spoken by The Most High God of Abraham, Isaac, and Jacob to the Israelites.

Exodus 20:2 I *am* the LORD thy God, which have brought thee out of the land of Egypt, out of the house of bondage.

The Most High identified Himself as the GOD, specific to the Israelites. He delivered the Israelites out of Egypt, not the descendants of Ishmael, Esau, Moab, or Ammon. The God of Israel will now tell His People how they should show Him LOVE.

Exodus 20:3 Thou shalt have no other gods before me.

The GOD of Our Fathers told us that He does not want us putting Allah, White Jesus, Buddha, Christmas trees, Easter Eggs, Easter bunny, New Years, etc. before Him.

Deuteronomy 7:25 The graven images of their gods shall ye burn with fire: thou shalt not desire the silver or gold *that is* on them, nor take *it* unto thee, lest thou be snared therein: for it *is* an abomination to the LORD thy God.

The Most High said it in His Laws not to have graven images. In case you have graven images, burn them with fire. Graven images are disgusting to Our GOD.

Deuteronomy 7:26 Neither shalt thou bring an abomination into thine house, lest thou be a cursed thing like it: *but* thou shalt utterly detest it, and thou shalt utterly abhor it; for it *is* a cursed thing.

The BLOOD of The Covenants

These Laws and Commandments were not given to the entire world, but to the Israelites. Our God never wanted us to Love the things in the world. You are not to celebrate Halloween, Thanksgiving, Christmas, New Year's, Valentine's Day, Easter, etc. They are disgusting to Our GOD. The Israelites are supposed to HATE it, not CELEBRATE it.

Exodus 20:4 Thou shalt not make unto thee any graven image, or any likeness *of anything* that *is* in heaven above, or that *is* in the earth beneath, or that *is* in the water under the earth:

Graven images is against the Laws and Commandments that The Most High God of Israel gave to the Israelites. That symbol of a crescent moon and star is a likeness of something in heaven above, so is that fish used in Christianity, which is used in the water.

Exodus 20:5 Thou shalt not bow down thyself to them, nor serve them: for I the LORD thy God *am* a jealous God, visiting the iniquity of the fathers upon the children unto the third and fourth *generation* of them that hate me;

In particular, the Israelites are not to worship or serve them. When you go to the Islamic temple, or Christian Church, you are worshiping the Crescent Moon and Star, or the Fish. Israelites are also serving other gods when they celebrate these idolatrous holidays that our enemies have given us to celebrate. They are not ordained by The Most High God of Abraham, Isaac, and Jacob. You do not have to wonder why Israelite children are dying in the streets at a higher rate than the children of all the nations combined, because The Most High VISITS this SIN upon our CHILLDREN. These Laws are not for the entire world, but for those of the captivity.

Exodus 20:7 Thou shalt not take the name of the LORD thy God in vain; for the LORD will not hold him guiltless that taketh his name in vain.

The Most High God of Abraham, Isaac, and Jacob does not want the Israelites using or saying His Name. Why are you Hebrews placing so much energy into The Most High God's Name?

49

The BLOOD of The Covenants

Ecclesiasticus 23:9 Accustom not thy mouth to swearing; neither use thyself to the naming of the Holy One.

This is a Commandment that many Hebrews today break. The Most High God does not want Israelites using His Name in your daily life. You are a god and you should abide by the Laws, Statues, and Commandments of Our GOD.

Psalms 82:6 I have said, Ye *are* gods; and all of you *are* children of the most High.

Being a god means to follow the Laws, Statues, and Commandments of Our GOD as He commanded the Israelites in the beginning.

Exodus 20:8 Remember the sabbath day, to keep it holy.

The Sabbath Day is the seventh day of the week, which is Friday at sunset to Saturday at sunset, because the beginning of a new day is not at midnight.

Genesis 1:5 And God called the light Day, and the darkness he called Night. And the evening and the morning were the first day.

As a Hebrew, we must be DILIGENT in these scriptures, or either Israelites would be worshiping our GOD on Sunday, worshiping on Christmas, Thanksgiving, New Years, etc.

Exodus 20:12 Honor thy father and thy mother: that thy days may be long upon the land which the LORD thy God giveth thee.

Another reason Hebrews are dying young, when you Israelites disrespect your parents, or your elders

Exodus 20:13 Thou shalt not kill.

We do not know how to LOVE and RESPECT our own people, because many Hebrews load their weapons with the intentions of killing another Hebrew. Not only does murder entails physically killing, but also hating your Brother without cause.

The BLOOD of The Covenants

1 John 3:15 Whosoever hateth his brother is a murderer: and ye know that no murderer hath eternal life abiding in him.

When you hate your Brother, you are a murderer. This is not saying that you cannot get angry with your Brother or Sister, but staying angry is hatred.

Ephesians 4:26 Be ye angry, and sin not: let not the sun go down upon your wrath:

Do not let your ANGER turn to HATE.

Exodus 20:14 Thou shalt not commit adultery.

Our people are LAWLESS. They do not respect the boundaries of the Covenant between a man and a woman. A Hebrew would sleep with another man's wife, then rap about it on wax.

Exodus 20:15 Thou shalt not steal.

These are the RULES of GODLINESS. If you are a god, you should know how to communicate with other gods, who are obeying the Laws and Commandments of the Father.

Exodus 20:16 Thou shalt not bear false witness against thy neighbor.

Are we trying to be GODLY? Let us face it. We must evaluate ourselves according to the Law, Statues, and Commandments. These are all Laws to rules your life.

Exodus 20:17 Thou shalt not covet thy neighbor's house, thou shalt not covet thy neighbor's wife, nor his manservant, nor his maidservant, nor his ox, nor his ass, nor any thing that *is* thy neighbor's.

A Covetous spirit cause multiple SINS. When a Hebrew covets a man's wife, you make plans to commit adultery. When you covet your neighbor's things, you make plans to steal them, or even kill.

The BLOOD of The Covenants

The Covenant After the Laws

After The Most High gave us His Laws and Statues, He made a Covenant with the SEED of Abraham, the Sons of Jacob, as The Most High promised He would.

Who Did The Most High God Give the Law?

These things are IMPORTANT when you, as an Israelite, consider the God that you are serving. What do you know about GOD, and what do you know about yourself?

Exodus 24:3 And Moses came and told the people all the words of the LORD, and all the judgments: and all the people answered with one voice, and said, All the words which the LORD hath said will we do.

Moses came down from the mountain, told the Israelites ALL the Laws, and Commandments and ALL the Judgments that The Most High God gave Him. All the Israelites agreed to the Laws.

Exodus 24:4 And Moses wrote all the words of the LORD, and rose up early in the morning, and builded an altar under the hill, and twelve pillars, according to the twelve tribes of Israel.

Moses wrote the Law, prepared an ALTAR with twelve pillars, representing the twelve tribes of Israel. It did not have one tribe, not the Jewish.

Revelation 2:9 I know thy works, and tribulation, and poverty, (but thou art rich) and *I know* the blasphemy of them which say they are Jews, and are not, but *are* the synagogue of Satan.

I am simply showing you that what you are seeing today is FALSE. The Most High God's people are the descendants of Jacob.

Deuteronomy 32:9 For the LORD'S portion *is* his people; Jacob *is* the lot of his inheritance.

Jacob is the Lot of The Most High God's Inheritance. Those people who are calling themselves Jews do not descend from Jacob. They descend from Amalek, and Seir which are both descendants of Esau.

The BLOOD of The Covenants

Esau Is Not A Descendant of Jacob, But the Twin Brother of Jacob.

Jew is short for "JUDAH," a seed of Jacob. Judah is not a descendant of Esau. Let us look at some of the descendants of Esau, so that you Israelites can get a better UNDERSTANDING of the TRUTH.

1 Chronicles 1:35 The sons of Esau; Eliphaz, Reuel, and Jeush, and Jaalam, and Korah.

These are the sons of Esau.

1 Chronicles 1:36 The sons of Eliphaz; Teman, and Omar, Zephi, and Gatam, Kenaz, and Timna, and Amalek.

Amalek is a grandson of Esau. These were the people against the Israelites when we came out of Egypt

Amalek Has Always Hated The Most High God and His People.

These people never had respect for the God of Abraham, Isaac, and Jacob, or His people!

Deuteronomy 25:17 Remember what Amalek did unto thee by the way, when ye were come forth out of Egypt;

When the Israelites came out of slavery, they did not have a military. They knew who the Israelites were. Do you think that they were trying to put the Israelites back into slavery to build their nation, as they did in Egypt?

Deuteronomy 25:18 How he met thee by the way, and smote the hindmost of thee, *even* all *that were* feeble behind thee, when thou *wast* faint and weary; and he feared not God.

Amalek viciously attacked the Israelites, killing many of the weak who were not able to keep up who were in the rear, as they were retreating. They had no FEAR of the God of Abraham, Isaac, and Jacob in the wilderness, neither do they have Fear of TMH God today. Amalekites are in the power seat today, still hating The Most High God of Abraham, Isaac, and Jacob

Deuteronomy 25:19 Therefore it shall be, when the LORD thy God hath given thee rest from all thine enemies round about, in the land which the LORD thy God giveth thee *for* an inheritance to possess it, *that* thou shalt blot out the remembrance of Amalek from under heaven; thou shalt not forget *it*.

When The Most High God return to MERCY on Jacob, He will destroy Amalek and all of Esau.

Obadiah 1:18 And the house of Jacob shall be a fire, and the house of Joseph a flame, and the house of Esau for stubble, and they shall kindle in them, and devour them; and there shall not be *any* remaining of the house of Esau; for the LORD hath spoken *it*.

Amalek is still around. They know what this Bible says about their end and they have changed their identity, pretending to be Jews.

Let Us Not Forget About Seir

There are many tribes of Edomites, because Esau had five sons, and these sons had children.

Genesis 36:9 And these *are* the generations of Esau the father of the Edomites in mount Seir:

Esau is associated with the name Edom, and Seir, the land that The Most High gave Esau. We know that the Amaleks hate the Israelites. What about the rest of the Edomites; do they Hate the Israelites.

Does Seir Hate the Israelites?

Let us examine what The Most High God thinks. Israelites who do not study the Precepts of this Bible can easily get led astray by doctrine of men.

Ezekiel 35:2 Son of man, set thy face against mount Seir, and prophesy against it,

The BLOOD of The Covenants

Seir represents the WHOLE nation of Edom, the people who like RED, RAW MEAT.

Genesis 25:30 And Esau said to Jacob, Feed me, I pray thee, with that same red *pottage*; for I *am* faint: therefore was his name called Edom.

That stew becomes RED when you throw the RAW meat into it, until the BLOOD cooks out. Esau likes his meat RAW.

Ezekiel 35:3 And say unto it, Thus saith the Lord GOD; Behold, O mount Seir, I *am* against thee, and I will stretch out mine hand against thee, and I will make thee most desolate.

This is a Prophesy that The Most High God showed the **Prophet Ezekiel** concerning Edom, when they were not the WORLD power. During this time, the Babylonians were the World power.

Ezekiel 35:4 I will lay thy cities waste, and thou shalt be desolate, and thou shalt know that I *am* the LORD.

Edomite cities have not been laid waste yet.

Malachi 1:2 I have loved you, saith the LORD. Yet ye say, Wherein hast thou loved us? *Was* not Esau Jacob's brother? saith the LORD: yet I loved Jacob,

The Most High God has a Favorite Son: Jacob. He Loved Jacob.

Malachi 1:3 And I hated Esau, and laid his mountains and his heritage waste for the dragons of the wilderness.

He also HATED ESAU, and He destroyed the inheritance, Mount Seir, that He gave them.

Malachi 1:4 Whereas Edom saith, We are impoverished, but we will return and build the desolate places; thus saith the LORD of hosts, They shall build, but I will throw down; and they shall call them, The border of wickedness, and, The people against whom the LORD hath indignation forever.

The BLOOD of The Covenants

Renaissance means REBIRTH, when the Edomites gained power and took control of the world, changing the faces of the JUDGES.

Job 9:24 The earth is given into the hand of the wicked: he covereth the faces of the judges thereof; if not, where, *and* who *is* he?

When the Edomites REBUILT their Kingdom, The Most High God, Christ, Moses, and all the Saints became White, and the Sons of Jacob became Heathens.

Ezekiel 35:5 Because thou hast had a perpetual hatred, and hast shed *the blood of* the children of Israel by the force of the sword in the time of their calamity, in the time *that their* iniquity *had* an end:

Who has hated so-called Blacks and Hispanics more than this so-called White man, not just in the present-day, but in the past also? As the Bible reveals that Esau HATED us, had no pity on us, when we were leaving slavery. These are the same people who did not have pity on us when the Israelites departed slavery in America. They created Laws to return the Israelites back into slavery.

Ezekiel 35:6 Therefore, *as* I live, saith the Lord GOD, I will prepare thee unto blood, and blood shall pursue thee: sith thou hast not hated blood, even blood shall pursue thee.

Since Esau likes killing The Most High God's people, there will come a time when DEATH pursues them. The hand of TMH God will be HEAVY against Esau.

Ezekiel 35:7 Thus will I make mount Seir most desolate, and cut off from it him that passeth out and him that returneth.

When this day happens, Edomite nations will no longer be trading centers of the world.

Our Subject Matter Was Who Did TMH Give the Law

I took the scenic route to show you that the same people who were standing in the way of Freedom when the Israelites departed Egypt are the same people standing in the way, blocking our freedoms today.

The BLOOD of The Covenants

Exodus 24:5 And he sent young men of the children of Israel, which offered burnt offerings, and sacrificed peace offerings of oxen unto the LORD.

During preparation for the first Covenant, it required a lot of BLOOD. Moses sent young Israelite men to offer PEACE OFFERINGS unto The Most High God of Abraham, Isaac, and Jacob.

Exodus 24:6 And Moses took half of the blood, and put *it* in basons; and half of the blood he sprinkled on the altar.

These huge basins are similar to large containers. They were filled with blood of oxen that were sacrificed in preparation of the Covenant.

Exodus 24:7 And he took the book of the covenant, and read in the audience of the people: and they said, All that the LORD hath said will we do, and be obedient.

This is the Covenant being performed. Moses read out of the Book of the Covenant, and the Israelites agreed to it. This is similar to us reading a contract and putting your signature on it, which is your way of saying that you agree to the terms of the contract.

Exodus 24:8 And Moses took the blood, and sprinkled *it* on the people, and said, Behold the blood of the covenant, which the LORD hath made with you concerning all these words.

That Blood was sprinkled on Israelites ONLY. How can you add yourself to a Contract or Agreement that does not include you? This was a BLOOD Covenant that was made between those who came out of Egypt. The characteristic of those people claiming to be Jews does not match the people of the Bible.

Exodus 24:9 Then went up Moses, and Aaron, Nadab, and Abihu, and seventy of the elders of Israel:

After the BLOOD Covenant with the Israelites, Moses, Aaron, Nadab, Abihu, and seventy Elders of Israel went up into Mount Sinai, the Mountain of The Most High God.

The BLOOD of The Covenants

Exodus 24:10 And they saw the God of Israel: and *there was* under his feet as it were a paved work of a sapphire stone, and as it were the body of heaven in *his* clearness.

You cannot claim that nobody ever saw The Most High God of the Israelites, when the Scriptures shows that Moses, Aaron, Nadab, Abihu and seventy Elders VIRTUALLY saw The Most High standing on paved rocks of Sapphire stone, as clear as day.

Exodus 24:11 And upon the nobles of the children of Israel he laid not his hand: also they saw God, and did eat and drink.

Also, the nobles' children sneaked up, and The Most High did not punish them. They also saw the GOD of Abraham, Isaac, and Jacob. Although The Most High was not Physically present, but they virtually saw Him as clear as day, and they sat down and did eat and drink in His presence. No other nation can make this claim, that they sat and ate with the GOD of Our fathers.

Exodus 24:12 And the LORD said unto Moses, Come up to me into the mount, and be there: and I will give thee tables of stone, and a law, and commandments which I have written; that thou mayest teach them.

The tables of stone did not include only the Ten Commandments, but also the Law, written at the Hands of The Most High God.

Out of All the People, TMH Chose the Israelites.
The God of the Heavens and Earth, of ALL Spirits created all nations, but He has a favorite!

2 Esdras 5:23 And said, O Lord that bearest rule, of every wood of the earth, and of all the trees thereof, thou hast chosen thee one only vine:

Out of all the trees that The Most High created, He has chosen One Vine.

The BLOOD of The Covenants

2 Esdras 5:24 And of all lands of the whole world thou hast chosen thee one pit: and of all the flowers thereof one lily:

Out of all the lands, The Most High has chosen one Land, where He created the garden of Eden. Out of all the flowers, TMH chose the lily. This shows that The Most High God of Abraham, Isaac, and Jacob has preferences, which are His favorites.

2 Esdras 5:25 And of all the depths of the sea thou hast filled thee one river: and of all builded cities thou hast hallowed Sion unto thyself:

He has a favorite body of water, a favorite city, which is Jerusalem. It is not Mecca, nor is it Rome. Let The Most High God tell you what He likes.

2 Esdras 5:26 And of all the fowls that are created thou hast named thee one dove: and of all the cattle that are made thou hast provided thee one sheep:

The Most High God has a favorite Bird. It is NOT the EAGLE! It is the DOVE. Of all the CATTLE, The Most High God chose the SHEEP. We are not supposed to worship the calf, or the cow, as some religions do. That is not the GOD of Abraham, Isaac, and Jacob's favorite.

2 Esdras 5:27 And among all the multitudes of people thou hast gotten thee one people: and unto this people, whom thou lovedst, thou gavest a law that is approved of all.

Of all the nations, The Most High God chose ONE people that He gave a LAW. Who did The Most High Give the Law?

2 Esdras 5:28 And now, O Lord, why hast thou given this one people over unto many? and upon the one root hast thou prepared others, and why hast thou scattered thy only one people among many?

Why has The Most High God given His Sons over to the other nations?

The BLOOD of The Covenants

The BLOOD of The Covenants

Chapter 8: The Conditions of the Agreement

The Most High God of Abraham, Isaac, and Jacob did not simply give the SEED of Abraham an OPEN AGREEMENT, where they are free to do whatever they want. He gave them CONDITIONS. The children of Israel will be BLESSED if they OBEY His Laws, Statues and Commandments, and they will get CURSES if they do not follow the Laws, Statues, and Commandments

Blessings For OBEDIENCE
Consider the entire of **Deuteronomy 28th** chapter the wedding vows between a Husband (Our GOD) and a Bride (Israel). The Most High God GUARANTEES that the SEED of Abraham, Isaac, and Jacob would be blessed ABOVE all nations if the Israelites OBEYED His VOICE and His Covenant.

Deuteronomy 28:1 And it shall come to pass, if thou shalt hearken diligently unto the voice of the LORD thy God, to observe *and* to do all his commandments which I command thee this day, that the LORD thy God will set thee on high above all nations of the earth:

Many Israelites REPENT, but are not thoroughly listening, or following the Laws of the GOD of Abraham, Isaac, and Jacob. We MUST observe and DO ALL the Commandments that The Most High commanded us. We cannot pick the Laws and Commandment that we like and reject those that we dislike.

Deuteronomy 28:2 And all these blessings shall come on thee, and overtake thee, if thou shalt hearken unto the voice of the LORD thy God.

All the Israelites, the SEED of Abraham, Isaac, and Jacob, have to do is OBEY His Voice and DO ALL Our GOD Commands us to do.

Deuteronomy 28:3 Blessed *shalt* thou *be* in the city, and blessed *shalt* thou *be* in the field.

We will be blessed everywhere we live.

The BLOOD of The Covenants

Deuteronomy 28:4 Blessed *shall be* the fruit of thy body, and the fruit of thy ground, and the fruit of thy cattle, the increase of thy kine, and the flocks of thy sheep.

Our children will be blessed, we would own land and farms, and all our crops and animals would be blessed.

Deuteronomy 28:5 Blessed *shall be* thy basket and thy store.

We would own storehouse to hold our things. That would be full, also our baskets that we carry goods will be blessed.

Deuteronomy 28:6 Blessed *shalt* thou *be* when thou comest in, and blessed *shalt* thou *be* when thou goest out.

We would be blessed when we are born and when we die.

Deuteronomy 28:7 The LORD shall cause thine enemies that rise up against thee to be smitten before thy face: they shall come out against thee one way, and flee before thee seven ways.

The Most High will destroy ALL of our ENEMIES that come against us, and we will pursue. Because the Israelites have REBELLED against Our GOD for so long, we have no idea what these blessings are as a people.

Deuteronomy 28:8 The LORD shall command the blessing upon thee in thy storehouses, and in all that thou settest thine hand unto; and he shall bless thee in the land which the LORD thy God giveth thee.

Everything that we set our hand to do will be blessed. The Most High will bless us in all the lands that He gave us.

Deuteronomy 28:9 The LORD shall establish thee an holy people unto himself, as he hath sworn unto thee, if thou shalt keep the commandments of the LORD thy God, and walk in his ways.

All the Israelites have to do is MAINTAIN the COVENANT that our forefathers made with the GOD of Abraham, Isaac, and Jacob and

The BLOOD of The Covenants

ALL our ENEMIES would know that the Israelites are the HOLY people of GOD.

Deuteronomy 28:13 And the LORD shall make thee the head, and not the tail; and thou shalt be above only, and thou shalt not be beneath; if that thou hearken unto the commandments of the LORD thy God, which I command thee this day, to observe and to do *them*:

The Israelites will be the HEAD everywhere. We would be HEADS of Governments, heads of state, heads of cities, etc.

Deuteronomy 28:14 And thou shalt not go aside from any of the words which I command thee this day, *to* the right hand, or *to* the left, to go after other gods to serve them.

The only thing that The Most High God wants us to do is to be GOOD CHILDREN.

These Blessings Is Because The Most High God Always LOVED Israel

The GOD of Abraham, Isaac, and Jacob LOVED the Israelites, before they came into existence, when he told Abraham that He will deliver them out of BONDAGE and give them the Hamites' land.

Deuteronomy 7:6 For thou *art* an holy people unto the LORD thy God: the LORD thy God hath chosen thee to be a special people unto himself, above all people that *are* upon the face of the earth.

Holy - dedicated or consecrated to God or a religious purpose; sacred.

The seed of Abraham, Isaac, and Jacob are a set-apart people to OUR GOD. He chose the Israelites to HIMSELF out of ALL the nations, and He placed us ABOVE ALL PEOPLE. The Israelites did not vote us to be above all people on the face of the Earth.

Deuteronomy 7:7 The LORD did not set his love upon you, nor choose you, because ye were more in number than any people; for ye *were* the fewest of all people:

The BLOOD of The Covenants

When The Most High chose the Israelites, we were the smallest nation. When the Israelites came into Egypt, we were only seventy in number.

Deuteronomy 7:8 But because the LORD loved you, and because he would keep the oath which he had sworn unto your fathers, hath the LORD brought you out with a mighty hand, and redeemed you out of the house of bondmen, from the hand of Pharaoh king of Egypt.

The LORD LOVED us, and He kept the OATH that He made with Abraham, Isaac, and Jacob, and The Most High brought us out of Egypt with a mighty hand, We were SAVED then and the same people will be SAVED in the future.

Deuteronomy 7:9 Know therefore that the LORD thy God, he *is* God, the faithful God, which keepeth covenant and mercy with them that love him and keep his commandments to a thousand generations;

The Most High God of Abraham, Isaac, and Jacob is a FAITHFUL GOD. He maintained a PROMISE with Abraham, even after he was dead and buried, and He is still maintaining a Covenant with us.

Deuteronomy 7:10 And repayeth them that hate him to their face, to destroy them: he will not be slack to him that hateth him, he will repay him to his face.

This is a warning to the children of Israel. The Most High is extremely LOYAL. Although the children of Israel have not maintained their side of the deal, He still has not cast away His people.

Romans 11:1 I say then, Hath God cast away his people? God forbid. For I also am an Israelite, of the seed of Abraham, *of* the tribe of Benjamin.

The Most High have not thrown us away, even though the Israelites have lost their way and many do not believe in Him

Deuteronomy 7:11 Thou shalt therefore keep the commandments, and the statutes, and the judgments, which I command thee this day, to do them.

The BLOOD of The Covenants

In a marriage, the husband demands that His wife follows and obeys Him, keep His Laws, and understand that there are penalty for breaking His Laws

Deuteronomy 7:12 Wherefore it shall come to pass, if ye hearken to these judgments, and keep, and do them, that the LORD thy God shall keep unto thee the covenant and the mercy which he sware unto thy fathers:

The reason The Most High is not Blessing us is because the Israelites are not keeping our side of the agreement. Sure, we have FREE will, but there are consequences for doing so, especially when the Israelites act outside the Covenant.

Deuteronomy 7:13 And he will love thee, and bless thee, and multiply thee: he will also bless the fruit of thy womb, and the fruit of thy land, thy corn, and thy wine, and thine oil, the increase of thy kine, and the flocks of thy sheep, in the land which he sware unto thy fathers to give thee.

All the Israelites have to do is OBEY Our Husband, because He is married to us.

Jeremiah 3:14 Turn, O backsliding children, saith the LORD; for I am married unto you: and I will take you one of a city, and two of a family, and I will bring you to Zion:

The Israelites makes a bad spouse, but we get really upset when our friends and family are not LOYAL.

Deuteronomy 7:14 Thou shalt be blessed above all people: there shall not be male or female barren among you, or among your cattle.

This is LOVE. The Israelites will be BLESSED ABOVE ALL PEOPLE. We would still have land, our wives, and our livestock shall not be barren in our lands.

The BLOOD of The Covenants

Curses or Evil Things For DISOBEDIENCE

There is a FLIPSIDE to this COVENANT that the Israelites are presently living today, because we definitely are not OBEDIENT to Our GOD. Of The Most High GOD's Ten Commandments, the majority of ALL Israelites obey less than four.

Deuteronomy 28:15 But it shall come to pass, if thou wilt not hearken unto the voice of the LORD thy God, to observe to do all his commandments and his statutes which I command thee this day; that all these curses shall come upon thee, and overtake thee:

If the Israelites do not want to HEAR, and DO ALL the LAWS, STATUES AND COMMANDMENTS of the God of Abraham, Isaac, and Jacob, then all these CURSES shall come upon the Israelites. Here are only a few of the CURSES. If The Most High God is CURSING His people, then He definitely is not BLESSING them. The presence of CURSES eliminates UNCONDITIONAL LOVE.

Deuteronomy 28:16 Cursed *shalt* thou *be* in the city, and cursed *shalt* thou *be* in the field.

Every Israelite community, ghetto, HOOD, barrio, where they inhabit by the majority, that community will be cursed with murder, drugs, prostitution, gang violence, high crime and high disease areas. It is no different in smaller cities either. This is not a BLESSING, or unconditional Love.

Deuteronomy 28:17 Cursed *shall be* thy basket and thy store.

The Israelites do not control anything in their communities, including their groceries they buy and the stores where the food is purchased. We are buying and eating harmful foods that our enemies are knowingly selling Israelites.

Ezekiel 4:13 And the LORD said, Even thus shall the children of Israel eat their defiled bread among the Gentiles, whither I will drive them.

The BLOOD of The Covenants

When the Israelites have no control of what is being produced and delivered for sale in the stores in communities that they inhabit, then they will be subjected to anything their enemies plan. Israelites have zero input regarding the harmful chemicals that our ENEMIES are allowing in the foods that they eat and the harmful effects

Deuteronomy 28:19 Cursed *shalt* thou *be* when thou comest in, and cursed *shalt* thou *be* when thou goest out.

The Israelites are CURSED when they are born, coming into the world and CURSED when they DIE, going out of the world, because they do not want to OBEY their GOD.

Deuteronomy 28:23 And thy heaven that *is* over thy head shall be brass, and the earth that is under thee *shall be* iron.

Israelites are still being subjected to slavery. Our ENEMIES have created a SCHOOL to PRISON PIPELINE, aimed directly at Israelites. Under the 13th Amendment, slavery was abolished, UNLESS imprisoned. We are the minorities in this land, but Israelites fill up the prison houses.

Isaiah 42:22 But this *is* a people robbed and spoiled; *they are* all of them snared in holes, and they are hid in prison houses: they are for a prey, and none delivereth; for a spoil, and none saith, Restore.

Israelites locked up in prison represent a CURSES, not unconditional love. There is not one country that has come to assist the Israelites in their struggles, not even the so-called leaders.

Deuteronomy 28:43 The stranger that *is* within thee shall get up above thee very high; and thou shalt come down very low.

When the Israelites had the rule, these nations or strangers were among us, serving as our servants.

Leviticus 25:45 Moreover of the children of the strangers that do sojourn among you, of them shall ye buy, and of their families that *are*

with you, which they begat in your land: and they shall be your possession.

These strangers who were the Israelites' possessions when The Most High God of Abraham, Isaac, and Jacob BLESSED us. Now, that the Israelites are CURSED, these strangers are lords over us.

2 Esdras 6:57 And now, O Lord, behold, these heathen, which have ever been reputed as nothing, have begun to be lords over us, and to devour us.

These strangers have now become lords over us and are devouring the Israelites. This is also part of the CURSES. We are no longer the HEAD, but are the TAIL.

Deuteronomy 28:44 He shall lend to thee, and thou shalt not lend to him: he shall be the head, and thou shalt be the tail.

Not having our own BANKS and lending institutions that lend to everybody is not a blessing but is a CURSE. When I hear many Israelites say that they are "too blessed to be stressed," simply means that they have become too comfortable in these CURSES.

Deuteronomy 28:48 Therefore shalt thou serve thine enemies which the LORD shall send against thee, in hunger, and in thirst, and in nakedness, and in want of all *things*: and he shall put a yoke of iron upon thy neck, until he have destroyed thee.

Right now, the Israelites are serving their ENEMIES, sent by the GOD of Abraham, Isaac, and Jacob. Our enemies supply us the defiled bread that we eat, everything we drink, and every garment that we wear, and everything else that we do. This enemy has become our god. Why? This enemy destroyed our minds, ability to read and write, and the knowledge of self and knowledge of the God of Abraham, Isaac, and Jacob.

Deuteronomy 28:54 *So that* the man *that is* tender among you, and very delicate, his eye shall be evil toward his brother, and toward the wife of his bosom, and toward the remnant of his children which he shall leave:

Gang violence is a CURSE. Our brothers, who we once loved, have now become an enemy because of the color of their flag or handkerchief. Many of these men create a family with a woman, and he disappears and leaves them. This is not a blessing in Israelite communities, but a CURSE. All of the events that are happening in Israelite communities can be associated with a CURSE.

Deuteronomy 28:61 Also every sickness, and every plague, which *is* not written in the book of this law, them will the LORD bring upon thee, until thou be destroyed.

High blood pressure, heart disease, high cholesterol, gout, AIDS and CRACK epidemic, etc. is not part of the Bible, but these disease have been brought upon the Israelites until we are destroyed. However, many Israelites do not know that they are spiritually DEAD.

Proverbs 21:16 The man that wandereth out of the way of understanding shall remain in the congregation of the dead.

When an Israelite has a HEATHEN mindset, having no UNDERSTANDING of their God, then he or she is SPIRITUALLY DEAD.

Deuteronomy 28:64 And the LORD shall scatter thee among all people, from the one end of the earth even unto the other; and there thou shalt serve other gods, which neither thou nor thy fathers have known, *even* wood and stone.

The Israelites were scattered in the Sub-Saharan slave trade by the Arabs and the Trans-Atlantic slave trade, gathered up by African ethnic groups and Arabs and sold to the White man.

How Were the Israelites Scattered?
I need to answer these questions that the scriptures impose, because this is how you are meant to learn.

The BLOOD of The Covenants

Joel 3:4 Yea, and what have ye to do with me, O Tyre, and Zidon, and all the coasts of Palestine? will ye render me a recompence? and if ye recompense me, swiftly *and* speedily will I return your recompence upon your own head;

Tyre and Zidon (or Sidon) refer to Canaanite nations and the Coast of Palestine or ancient Philistine or Hamite people. The Most High is asking these nations what have they to do with Him? Were they attempting to punish The Most High through punishing His people?

Joel 3:5 Because ye have taken my silver and my gold, and have carried into your temples my goodly pleasant things:

They took the silver and gold out of His Temple and carried it into their temples.

Joel 3:6 The children also of Judah and the children of Jerusalem have ye sold unto the Grecians, that ye might remove them far from their border.

They gathered up all of the Jews and sold them to the White man to remove us out of the land. They thought that their life would be much better without us. This is how we were scattered among the nations, because those slave ships carried the Israelites into many lands.

Deuteronomy 28:65 And among these nations shalt thou find no ease, neither shall the sole of thy foot have rest: but the LORD shall give thee there a trembling heart, and failing of eyes, and sorrow of mind:

Israelites are not living an easy life in any of these nations. It is rough in the hoods in Europe where Israelites dwell as it is in America

Deuteronomy 28:66 And thy life shall hang in doubt before thee; and thou shalt fear day and night, and shalt have none assurance of thy life:

There is no guarantee of an Israelite's life. He can be walking home from work, waiting on a train to go home, or pulled over by a trigger-happy and racist policeman and killed.

The BLOOD of The Covenants

Deuteronomy 28:68 And the LORD shall bring thee into Egypt again with ships, by the way whereof I spake unto thee, Thou shalt see it no more again: and there ye shall be sold unto your enemies for bondmen and bondwomen, and no man shall buy *you.*

"Egypt" represents BONDAGE

Deuteronomy 5:6 I *am* the LORD thy God, which brought thee out of the land of Egypt, from the house of bondage.

The God of Abraham, Isaac, and Jacob will BRING us into SLAVERY with SHIPS. This means that we will not stay in the land, that The Most High will bring us OUT of the Land with ships, and we will be sold to our ENEMIES. Does the White man have a FRIENDLY history with the so-called Blacks, Hispanics, and Native Americans? The White man began the Trans-Atlantic Slave Trade with Christopher Columbus on October 12, 1492. The so-called White man is OUR ENEMY. What about the Arabs, do they have a FRIENDLY relationship against us? Their so-called prophet Mohammad started the Sub-Saharan slave trade, selling Jews, the tribes of Judah, Benjamin and Levi, all over the world, to the four corners of the earth.. The Arabs are our ENEMIES.

The Most High Laid Out the Agreement Before Us.
The Most High laid everything out before the children of Israel, the SEED of Abraham, Isaac, and Jacob.

Deuteronomy 11:26 Behold, I set before you this day a blessing and a curse;

The Most High gave us the stipulation whether the Israelite want to CHOOSE the Blessings by OBEYING His Laws, Statues and Commandments, or Do Evil and CHOOSE the CURSES. He told the Israelites the result when they chose either one. The Israelites, as well as all people have CHOICE to be GOOD or EVIL, but The Most High chose ONLY ONE nation of people.

The BLOOD of The Covenants

Deuteronomy 11:27 A blessing, if ye obey the commandments of the LORD your God, which I command you this day:

The stipulation of this Covenant is all the Blessing if the Israelites OBEY His Voice and DO His WILL

Deuteronomy 11:28 And a curse, if ye will not obey the commandments of the LORD your God, but turn aside out of the way which I command you this day, to go after other gods, which ye have not known.

The Sons of Jacob will receive EVIL THINGS, or CURSES if they DISOBEY His VOICE and NOT DO ALL His Laws, Statues, and Commandments.

The BLOOD of The Covenants

Chapter 9: The Most High Appoints the Levites to Be Mediators of the Old Covenant.

After The Covenant was created, The Most High appointed the Levites to be the Mediators of the Old Covenant, to hear the SINS of the Israelites, receive offering of a Lamb, Goat, Bullock, etc., sacrifice it for the remission of certain SINS. The BLOOD of Animals could not free you from ALL sins, only certain sins.

Numbers 3:5 And the LORD spake unto Moses, saying,

Numbers 3:6 Bring the tribe of Levi near, and present them before Aaron the priest, that they may minister unto him.

The Most High God chose the Tribe of Levi to minister, which means to serve.. This tribe had multiple roles. They were responsible for the keep of the tabernacle, the HOLIEST of Holy places, and making sacrifices for the entire nation of the children of Israel for the forgiveness of SIN. They were also keepers of the LAW.

Malachi 2:7 For the priest's lips should keep knowledge, and they should seek the law at his mouth: for he *is* the messenger of the LORD of hosts.

Understanding the ROLE and the structure of the nation of Israel, which was established by The Most High God of Abraham, Isaac, and Jacob. The Levites taught the Law and gave instruction in the Law. The Most High chose His Prophets to WARN the Israelites when they went astray, distinct roles.

Ezekiel 3:11 And go, get thee to them of the captivity, unto the children of thy people, and speak unto them, and tell them, Thus saith the Lord GOD; whether they will hear, or whether they will forbear.

The Prophets came on behalf of The Most High God when the Priest went astray or the children of Israel went astray, rebuking them because they are violating the Laws of their GOD.

The BLOOD of The Covenants

Numbers 3:7 And they shall keep his charge, and the charge of the whole congregation before the tabernacle of the congregation, to do the service of the tabernacle.

They will be responsible for themselves and for ALL the Tribes, and they will perform the SERVICE of the Tabernacle, responsible for all the things pertaining to The Most High God of Abraham, Isaac, and Jacob..

Numbers 3:8 And they shall keep all the instruments of the tabernacle of the congregation, and the charge of the children of Israel, to do the service of the tabernacle.

The Levites will be responsible for all the instruments of the tabernacle and responsible for the children of Israel. We will later understand what the service of the tabernacle.

Numbers 3:9 And thou shalt give the Levites unto Aaron and to his sons: they *are* wholly given unto him out of the children of Israel.

The Most High God placed the Levites under Aaron and his sons. All of the tribe of Levi came out of the Sons of Jacob. They did not come from other nations. In other words, it is a family affair. I am starting from the Genesis of what the First Mediators jobs were, and what was included in this position..

Numbers 3:10 And thou shalt appoint Aaron and his sons, and they shall wait on their priest's office: and the stranger that cometh nigh shall be put to death.

When The Most High established the Priest position, any nation that came near the tabernacle was commanded by The Most High that they be put to death.

Numbers 1:51 And when the tabernacle setteth forward, the Levites shall take it down: and when the tabernacle is to be pitched, the Levites shall set it up: and the stranger that cometh nigh shall be put to death.

The BLOOD of The Covenants

This Covenant is EXCLUSIVE to the Israelites, such that The Most High did not want the other nations to come near Him.

Numbers 3:11 And the LORD spake unto Moses, saying,

Numbers 3:12 And I, behold, I have taken the Levites from among the children of Israel instead of all the firstborn that openeth the matrix among the children of Israel: therefore the Levites shall be mine;

Prior to The Most High taking the Levites as His, He took the Firstborn from among the Israelites. As a husband to the Israelites, The Most High took care of the Levites.

The Most High Set Up A System Inside Israel to Take Care of the Levites

When The Most High took the Tribe of Levi to Himself, He created Laws and Statues to ensure that the Levites would be taken care of.

Deuteronomy 18:1 The priests the Levites, *and* all the tribe of Levi, shall have no part nor inheritance with Israel: they shall eat the offerings of the LORD made by fire, and his inheritance.

The Most High God did not give the Tribe of Levi any land, when He divided the land among the other eleven tribes. He also gave them part of His burnt offerings made by fire.

The Offering Made By Fire

Sacrifices were made every day and the Levites did eat of the animals that they sacrificed.

Leviticus 7:1 Likewise this *is* the law of the trespass offering: it *is* most holy.

This was the Law of The Old Covenant for unintentional or intentional transgressions, which is called the TREPASS offering.

Leviticus 7:2 In the place where they kill the burnt offering shall they kill the trespass offering: and the blood thereof shall he sprinkle round about upon the altar.

The BLOOD of The Covenants

They killed the trespass offering in the same place as the burnt offering, and they shall sprinkle the blood on the altar.

Leviticus 7:3 And he shall offer of it all the fat thereof; the rump, and the fat that covereth the inwards,

The Levites shall offer ALL the fat, the rump and the fat covering the inwards. That is not the entire animal.

Leviticus 7:4 And the two kidneys, and the fat that *is* on them, which *is* by the flanks, and the caul *that is* above the liver, with the kidneys, it shall he take away:

The kidneys, fat that is on the kidneys, the caul, or membrane above the liver, does not get sacrificed. The Levites were commanded to take that away.

Leviticus 7:5 And the priest shall burn them upon the altar *for* an offering made by fire unto the LORD: it *is* a trespass offering.

The Priest shall burn the rump and the fat on the altar.

Leviticus 7:6 Every male among the priests shall eat thereof: it shall be eaten in the holy place: it *is* most holy.

Basically, the priest will cook the rump and the fat and every male among the Priest shall eat of this burnt offering. You noticed that there are no women in service to The Most High, or who were able to eat the sacrifice?

Numbers 27:16 Let the LORD, the God of the spirits of all flesh, set a man over the congregation,

The Most High God NEVER set a woman over His people. Furthermore, the meat is also eaten. It is like a holy barbeque. If we look at the holidays that our ENEMIES have given us, are we roasting, smoking, barbequing, baking some sort of meat?

The BLOOD of The Covenants

The Most High God Hate The Feast Days That We Are Celebrating in This Land.

All of these holidays, that the Israelites have been celebrating in the land that they are held captive, were not given to us by Our God, but by our ENEMIES.

Amos 5:21 I hate, I despise your feast days, and I will not smell in your solemn assemblies.

Thanksgiving, Christmas, Easter, Independence Day, The Most High hates these days. He did not give these days to worship and the Israelites are worshiping another god other than Him.

Exodus 34:14 For thou shalt worship no other god: for the LORD, whose name *is* Jealous, *is* a jealous God:

Our GOD is JEALOUS and He HATES when you serve other gods.

Amos 5:22 Though ye offer me burnt offerings and your meat offerings, I will not accept *them*: neither will I regard the peace offerings of your fat beasts.

When an Israelite has made himself ABOMINALE, worshiping The Most High will be in vain.

Leviticus 20:25 Ye shall therefore put difference between clean beasts and unclean, and between unclean fowls and clean: and ye shall not make your souls abominable by beast, or by fowl, or by any manner of living thing that creepeth on the ground, which I have separated from you as unclean.

Today, Hebrews want to pray over all types of meat, including hams, shrimps, crabs, lobsters, all types of pork, and unclean fish. That is ABOMINABLE, or disgusting to The Most High. It is easy to understand why He is not accepting the offering. If an Israelite put a difference between clean and unclean meats and worshiped the God of Abraham, Isaac, Jacob only, then He would be more accepting of us.

The BLOOD of The Covenants

Leviticus 20:26 And ye shall be holy unto me: for I the LORD *am* holy, and have severed you from *other* people, that ye should be mine.

There is a REQUIREMENT to be a god like your FATHER. You must be set apart. You cannot eat the same foods, there is a dress code. Israelites have a ROYAL lineage. CLAIM IT!

Amos 5:23 Take thou away from me the noise of thy songs; for I will not hear the melody of thy viols.

When Israelites are in these churches at Sunday worship, or early morning Christmas and Easter worship, you are worshiping another god. Your GOD does not want to hear that awful noise!

Amos 5:24 But let judgment run down as waters, and righteousness as a mighty stream.

For our actions, The Most High is destroying our sons and daughters, judging them in the Law.

Leviticus 7:7 As the sin offering *is*, so *is* the trespass offering: *there is* one law for them: the priest that maketh atonement therewith shall have *it*.

The SIN offering and the Trespass offering are the same. The Levite who make the atonement shall have the offering. The Levites only sacrificed the rump and the fat on the altar. The remaining of the animal belongs to the Priest who made the sacrifice.

Leviticus 7:8 And the priest that offereth any man's burnt offering, *even* the priest shall have to himself the skin of the burnt offering which he hath offered.

The hide of the animal also goes to the Priest. You should now be able to understand why the Leadership in Israel, especially the Priest, were against Christ. They saw the potential, or the effect of Christ winning over the Jew, making them a believer, that these Jews would no longer bring sacrifices to the Temple. The Priest made a living off of these sacrifices.

The BLOOD of The Covenants

Leviticus 7:9 And all the meat offering that is baken in the oven, and all that is dressed in the frying pan, and in the pan, shall be the priest's that offereth it.

All the meat offering that is baked or fried also belong to the Priest who offered it.

Leviticus 7:10 And every meat offering, mingled with oil, and dry, shall all the sons of Aaron have, one *as much* as another.

This meat offering mixed with oil or dry belong to the Sons of Aaron. It is divided equally.

Deuteronomy 18:2 Therefore shall they have no inheritance among their brethren: the LORD *is* their inheritance, as he hath said unto them.

The Levites did not get a possession of land as the other tribes, but their inheritance is The Most High.

Deuteronomy 18:3 And this shall be the priest's due from the people, from them that offer a sacrifice, whether *it be* ox or sheep; and they shall give unto the priest the shoulder, and the two cheeks, and the maw.

The priest get of every sacrifice the shoulder, two cheeks and the maw, or fourth stomach of a cow, which I used for making cheese.

Deuteronomy 18:4 The firstfruit *also* of thy corn, of thy wine, and of thine oil, and the first of the fleece of thy sheep, shalt thou give him.

There is a Law that The Most High called TITHE

Tithing Was Specifically for the Levites.

Tithing was created to take care of the Levites, because they did not have time to raise crops, tend to livestock, or make oils and wine, etc. Being in Service to The Most High means, to the Levites, they must sacrifice ALL the SIN offerings, Peace offerings, Trespass offerings, etc., and tend to the tabernacle each day.

The BLOOD of The Covenants

Deuteronomy 14:22 Thou shalt truly tithe all the increase of thy seed, that the field bringeth forth year by year.

Tithing was never about giving money to the pastor. The God of Our Fathers said we tithe, or give a tenth of whatever we grow with seed that the field produces each YEAR.

Deuteronomy 14:23 And thou shalt eat before the LORD thy God, in the place which he shall choose to place his name there, the tithe of thy corn, of thy wine, and of thine oil, and the firstlings of thy herds and of thy flocks; that thou mayest learn to fear the LORD thy God always.

We bring that Tithe and EAT before OUR GOD, as we did after He made a Covenant with us. We go before Him to Jerusalem with corn, wine, oil, the first of our herds, of our flock. To FEAR Our GOD means that ALL the SEEDS of Jacob MUST learn to OBEY Him. This shows that all of Israel gathered before Our GOD in Love, Peace, and Happiness! It shows us that when we had the God of Abraham, Isaac, and Jacob among us, the Israelites were able to gather without violence.

Deuteronomy 14:24 And if the way be too long for thee, so that thou art not able to carry it; *or* if the place be too far from thee, which the LORD thy God shall choose to set his name there, when the LORD thy God hath blessed thee:

If an Israelite family lived too far from Jerusalem, or you would not be able to carry all the tithes that The Most High God has blessed you with, then The Most High gave us SPECIAL INSTRUCTIONS. The Most High never wanted us to come to the party empty handed..

Deuteronomy 14:25 Then shalt thou turn *it* into money, and bind up the money in thine hand, and shalt go unto the place which the LORD thy God shall choose:

If it is too far, or too much to carry, then the Israelite shall SELL all of his tithes that he would deliver to Jerusalem for money. He take the money with him to Jerusalem. This is why it is always inappropriate to come to a gathering without bringing something to the gathering.

The BLOOD of The Covenants

These precepts teaches not only, about Tithing, but also how each family came to the gathering. The Tithe says that we should allocate ten percent, bring it to Jerusalem and eat before The Most High God AND give the Levite Priest their portion.

Deuteronomy 14:26 And thou shalt bestow that money for whatsoever thy soul lusteth after, for oxen, or for sheep, or for wine, or for strong drink, or for whatsoever thy soul desireth: and thou shalt eat there before the LORD thy God, and thou shalt rejoice, thou, and thine household,

When the Israelite gets to Jerusalem, he take the money and buy whatever he lusted after, like animals, wine, strong drink, sheep, etc. He take what he purchased and eat before The Most High God, him and his household.

Deuteronomy 14:27 And the Levite that *is* within thy gates; thou shalt not forsake him; for he hath no part nor inheritance with thee.

The TITHE is also for the Levites that works withing the tabernacles within the cities wherein that Israelite lives. It would be disrespectful to pay your tithing to Levites that take care of Hebrews in a different city. Israelites should pay tithes to the ones who were doing work in their city.

Deuteronomy 14:28 At the end of three years thou shalt bring forth all the tithe of thine increase the same year, and shalt lay *it* up within thy gates:

The TITHES were brought to the Levites within your city at the end of three years. The ORIGINAL TITHES was not money, and it was not paid to a Pastor, Preacher, Bishop, or Minister, but to a Tribe of Levi of the Sons of Jacob.

Deuteronomy 14:29 And the Levite, (because he hath no part nor inheritance with thee,) and the stranger, and the fatherless, and the widow, which *are* within thy gates, shall come, and shall eat and be satisfied; that the LORD thy God may bless thee in all the work of thine hand which thou doest.

The BLOOD of The Covenants

Not only was Tithing for the SUPPORT of the LEVITES, but it was also for the strangers, fatherless, and the widow within that city. This is when you see the WEALTH of a nation when that nation has a system in place that take care of ALL the people. Our GOD created a system to take care of the fatherless, widows, and strangers.

Deuteronomy 18:5 For the LORD thy God hath chosen him out of all thy tribes, to stand to minister in the name of the LORD, him and his sons forever.

The Levites were CHOSEN to SERVE in the Name of The Most High God of Abraham, Isaac, and Jacob, to be a MEDIATOR between the Israelites and The Most High. When The Most High CHOSE the Levites to be in service to Him, He created TITHING to take care of them. Tithing is NOT created to support the present day Pastor. They are NOT in service to the GOD of Abraham, Isaac, and Jacob.

The BLOOD of The Covenants

Chapter 10: When the Israelites Were Obedient, He Placed Us Above All Nations.

The Most High God made a Covenant with the Israelites, and He told them that if they OBEYED His Voice, He would place us ABOVE ALL people upon the face of the Earth.

King David Subdued All His Enemies

2 Samuel 8:1 And after this it came to pass, that David smote the Philistines, and subdued them: and David took Methegammah out of the hand of the Philistines.

King David subdued the Philistines

Metheg-ammah

Source: https://en.wikipedia.org/wiki/Metheg-ammah

The Pulpit Commentary argues that "Metheg-ammah means "the bridle of the mother city". We learn from the parallel place (1 Chronicles 18:1) that the city of Gath is meant by this phrase. Gath was at this time the metropolis of Philistia and had reduced the other four chief towns to a state of vassalage. Thus by taking Gath, his old city of refuge (1 Samuel 27:2), David acquired also the supremacy which he had previously exercised over the whole country"

This mega city was the Capital of the Philistines. Once King David captured this city, the Philistines were subdued.

King David subdued the Moabites

2 Samuel 8:2 And he smote Moab, and measured them with a line, casting them down to the ground; even with two lines measured he to put to death, and with one full line to keep alive. And *so* the Moabites became David's servants, *and* brought gifts.

The BLOOD of The Covenants

David line the Moabites up in two lines, one he killed the other, he left alive. They became his servants and paid him tribute.

2 Samuel 8:3 David smote also Hadadezer, the son of Rehob, king of Zobah, as he went to recover his border at the river Euphrates.

Hadadezer was a Syrian king. David also destroyed the Syrians. All the nations that the Israelites had fallen captive were subdued by King David, because The Most High God LOVED David, a man after His own heart.

Acts 13:22 And when he had removed him, he raised up unto them David to be their king; to whom also he gave testimony, and said, I have found David the *son* of Jesse, a man after mine own heart, which shall fulfil all my will.

The Most High God subdued all of King David's enemies, because He OBEDED the Voice of The Most High. This is evidence that The Most High LOVES those who love Him.

Proverbs 8:17 I love them that love me; and those that seek me early shall find me.

If you are not doing as The Most High commands, why should He show you love?

2 Samuel 8:4 And David took from him a thousand *chariots*, and seven hundred horsemen, and twenty thousand footmen: and David houghed all the chariot *horses*, but reserved of them *for* an hundred chariots.

Hough a horse - severing the Achilles tendon of the hind legs of captured horses, making them useless to the Israelites or their enemies as war horses (1 Chronicles 18:4).

David made all the Syrian horses useless for war except about a hundred

The BLOOD of The Covenants

2 Samuel 8:5 And when the Syrians of Damascus came to succor Hadadezer king of Zobah, David slew of the Syrians two and twenty thousand men.

When the Syrians of Damascus came to help Hadadezer, King David slew 22,000 men.

2 Samuel 8:6 Then David put garrisons in Syria of Damascus: and the Syrians became servants to David, *and* brought gifts. And the LORD preserved David whithersoever he went.

King David subdued the Syrians and made them Servants, placing his troops in a fortress in Damascus to defend it. This is the same concept that America uses.

2 Samuel 8:7 And David took the shields of gold that were on the servants of Hadadezer, and brought them to Jerusalem.

David took gold off Hadadezer's servants.

2 Samuel 8:8 And from Betah, and from Berothai, cities of Hadadezer, king David took exceeding much brass.

He also took an exceeding amount of brass from Betah and Berothai.

2 Samuel 8:9 When Toi king of Hamath heard that David had smitten all the host of Hadadezer,

2 Samuel 8:10 Then Toi sent Joram his son unto king David, to salute him, and to bless him, because he had fought against Hadadezer, and smitten him: for Hadadezer had wars with Toi. And *Joram* brought with him vessels of silver, and vessels of gold, and vessels of brass:

Toi, an enemy of Hadadezer also brough vessels of silver, gold, and brass to King David.

2 Samuel 8:11 Which also king David did dedicate unto the LORD, with the silver and gold that he had dedicated of all nations which he subdued.

King David dedicated all of this to The Most High God.

The BLOOD of The Covenants

2 Samuel 8:12 Of Syria, and of Moab, and of the children of Ammon, and of the Philistines, and of Amalek, and of the spoil of Hadadezer, son of Rehob, king of Zobah.

The Nations that King David subdued

- **Syria**
- **Moab**
- **Ammon**
- **Philistines**
- **Amalek**

2 Samuel 8:13 And David gat *him* a name when he returned from smiting of the Syrians in the valley of salt, *being* eighteen thousand *men*.

King David's name became great among men

King David also subdued Edom
King David placed fortress of men throughout the Edomite's land

2 Samuel 8:14 And he put garrisons in Edom; throughout all Edom put he garrisons, and all they of Edom became David's servants. And the LORD preserved David whithersoever he went.

Many things that the nations do today, they learned from the Israelites. King David placed MILITARY BASES in his enemies' land. The Israelites did it first.

Chapter 11: The Israelites Backslid Against The Most High And He Wanted to Know Why

The Most High God asked the children of Israel a question what has He done to the Israelites to make them want to follow other gods?

The Most High Wants to Know What is His Offense

Jeremiah 2:4 Hear ye the word of the LORD, O house of Jacob, and all the families of the house of Israel:

The Most High God is talking ONLY to HIS People, the twelve tribes of Israel

Jeremiah 2:5 Thus saith the LORD, What iniquity have your fathers found in me, that they are gone far from me, and have walked after vanity, and are become vain?

The Most High wants to know what sins our forefathers did find in Him. When the Israelites obeyed His Covenant, as King David, The Moat High Blessed the Israelites, making them the head and not the tail. Our forefathers were prideful, full of themselves, and so are we!

Jeremiah 2:6 Neither said they, Where *is* the LORD that brought us up out of the land of Egypt, that led us through the wilderness, through a land of deserts and of pits, through a land of drought, and of the shadow of death, through a land that no man passed through, and where no man dwelt?

Neither did our forefathers seek The Most High God who delivered them out of the land of Egypt, and led them through the wilderness, where no man ever lived.

Jeremiah 2:7 And I brought you into a plentiful country, to eat the fruit thereof and the goodness thereof; but when ye entered, ye defiled my land, and made mine heritage an abomination.

Neither did our forefathers seek the God of Abraham, Isaac and Jacob who brought us into the lands of Canaan, a bountiful land. When we entered the land, we defiled it, breaking the Covenant of The Most High. All the things

The BLOOD of The Covenants

that The Most High told us was an ABOMINATION to Him in His Covenant, His children are violating.

Jeremiah 2:8 The priests said not, Where *is* the LORD? and they that handle the law knew me not: the pastors also transgressed against me, and the prophets prophesied by Baal, and walked after *things that* do not profit.

The Priest and Leaders, those who are supposed to be responsible for the Law do not know The Most High.

Hosea 4:1 Hear the word of the LORD, ye children of Israel: for the LORD hath a controversy with the inhabitants of the land, because *there is* no truth, nor mercy, nor knowledge of God in the land.

These people who were supposed to know the Law, had no knowledge. Guess what? This is exactly how our leaders are established today. The majority of your Christian Leaders are preaching from doctrine that is not supported by the Bible.

Jeremiah 2:9 Wherefore I will yet plead with you, saith the LORD, and with your children's children will I plead.

When The Most High God PLEADS, He is not begging.

Isaiah 66:16 For by fire and by his sword will the LORD plead with all flesh: and the slain of the LORD shall be many.

You cannot blame Esau, Ishmael, Moab, Ammon, or even Jacob for the millions of Israelites that have been killed during slavery, and all the eras after slavery. The Most High God's heritage is ABOMINABLE! He is PLEADING, and the SLAIN of His people are MANY, and counting.

Jeremiah 2:10 For pass over the isles of Chittim, and see; and send unto Kedar, and consider diligently, and see if there be such a thing.

The Most High is telling the Jews how He will PLEAD with them: using Esau and the Ishmaelites.

The BLOOD of The Covenants

Chittim is Rome

Source: http://home.windstream.net/aj31401/Chittim.html

The country of Chittim, which is mentioned in the Book of Daniel, is not found anywhere else in the Bible, but it is found in the Book of Jasher. The verse below explains that the children of Chittim are the Romans that live in the valley of Canopia, which is by the Tiber River. The Romans, of course, live in the city of Rome, and the Tiber is the main river that runs through the city of Rome.

> Ja 10:16 And the children of Chittim are the Romim (Romans) who dwell in the valley of Canopia by the river Tibreu (Tiber).

Kedar is a Descendant of Ishmael

Genesis 25:13 And these *are* the names of the sons of Ishmael, by their names, according to their generations: the firstborn of Ishmael, Nebajoth; and Kedar, and Adbeel, and Mibsam,

The Jews were enslaved by the Romans and their descendants and the Ishmaelites and their descendants. Ishmaelites has enslaved the Jews for over 1400 years.

Jeremiah 2:11 Hath a nation changed *their* gods, which *are* yet no gods? but my people have changed their glory for *that which* doth not profit.

We have changed our gods to Allah, the crescent moon and star, and a Kaaba (black) stone. We have changed our god to the Christian Cross, and White Jesus. These religions have not profited us at all.

Jeremiah 2:12 Be astonished, O ye heavens, at this, and be horribly afraid, be ye very desolate, saith the LORD.

If we look at the atrocities that the people of the Bible have suffered and associate it with the ANGER of The Most High, we should be thinking on our ways and return to His Laws.

The BLOOD of The Covenants

Psalms 119:59 I thought on my ways, and turned my feet unto thy testimonies.

Because the people of The Most High God are too blind to see that their Elohim is ANGRY, and He is destroying them because of their ABOMINATIONS, they have not thought on their ways.

Jeremiah 2:13 For my people have committed two evils; they have forsaken me the fountain of living waters, *and* hewed them out cisterns, broken cisterns, that can hold no water.

The Most High God's people have committed two **evils (1)** We forsook The Most High God's Covenant. The doctrine that most of you are holding does not represent The Most High God. **(2)** We have replaced The Most High God's Covenant with Islam, Christianity, Egyptology, etc.

Jeremiah 2:14 *Is* Israel a servant? *is* he a homeborn *slave*? why is he spoiled?

Because the Israelites have FORSAKEN The Most High God, He has also FORSAKEN us. Yes, we are gods, ONLY when we do as The Most High God commanded.

Psalms 82:6 I have said, Ye *are* gods; and all of you *are* children of the most High.

Many of you Hebrews claiming to be a god do not qualify to be a god. Even The Most High God does not claim you, because His Heritage is an ABOMINATION!

Jeremiah 2:21 Yet I had planted thee a noble vine, wholly a right seed: how then art thou turned into the degenerate plant of a strange vine unto me?

The Most High gave us Laws, Statues and Commandments, planted us RIGHTEOUSLY. Yet we have become DEGENERATES! True, Israelites can become gods when they follow the instruction of The Most High God, their Father.

The BLOOD of The Covenants

The Pastors and Priest Also Betrayed the Covenant of The Most High

The Prophets and Pastors today have also betrayed the Covenant of The Most High. They have not RIGHTED the ship, guiding the children of Israel back to Their GOD.

Jeremiah 23:1 Woe be unto the pastors that destroy and scatter the sheep of my pasture! saith the LORD.

Woe means destruction. The Most High is talking to those who are supposed to be teaching and ministering the word, but are leading The Most High God's people astray

Jeremiah 23:2 Therefore thus saith the LORD God of Israel against the pastors that feed my people; Ye have scattered my flock, and driven them away, and have not visited them: behold, I will visit upon you the evil of your doings, saith the LORD.

The Most High God has a problem with you pastors today, scattering His people into all types of religions. The majority of pastors do not teach the Law, telling them the Laws are done away, and you welcome other nations and their money into your congregation

Jeremiah 23:9 Mine heart within me is broken because of the prophets; all my bones shake; I am like a drunken man, and like a man whom wine hath overcome, because of the LORD, and because of the words of his holiness.

Jeremiah is heartbroken, knowing what The Most High is about to do to His people because of the lying Prophets.

Jeremiah 23:10 For the land is full of adulterers; for because of swearing the land mourneth; the pleasant places of the wilderness are dried up, and their course is evil, and their force *is* not right.

People are cheating on The Most High God throughout the land

Jeremiah 23:11 For both prophet and priest are profane; yea, in my house have I found their wickedness, saith the LORD.

The BLOOD of The Covenants

Both the Prophets and Priests are profaning The Most High God's Laws and His people. They are in the church today still profaning His people

Ezekiel 22:26 Her priests have violated my law, and have profaned mine holy things: they have put no difference between the holy and profane, neither have they shewed *difference* between the unclean and the clean, and have hid their eyes from my sabbaths, and I am profaned among them.

This goes to show that the Jews did not know their Elohim then, nor do they know Him today. They still follow the same wicked Pastors, Prophets and Priests today. These people are not teaching the WILL of GOD, but from their own lustful thoughts!

Psalms 40:8 I delight to do thy will, O my God: yea, thy law *is* within my heart.

Instead, these pastors are saying Christ done away with the Laws of His Father

Jeremiah 23:12 Wherefore their way shall be unto them as slippery *ways* in the darkness: they shall be driven on, and fall therein: for I will bring evil upon them, *even* the year of their visitation, saith the LORD.

These wicked Pastors seem to be successful, profiting off of their people's backs, but their ways shall be like a slippery path in the dark. The Most High will bring EVIL upon them. You watch! All of these wicked men and women shall fall.

Jeremiah 23:13 And I have seen folly in the prophets of Samaria; they prophesied in Baal, and caused my people Israel to err.

The Most High is now talking about the foolishness of the Northern Kingdom Prophets who prophesied, not by The Most High, but by Baal, and caused the Northern Kingdom to err. All of these Christian Pastors today are prophesying by Baal, not according to The Most High God. They have a Bible, and they use a few unrelated verses for their sermon. This makes them FALSE PROPHETS.

The BLOOD of The Covenants

Jeremiah 23:<u>14</u> I have seen also in the prophets of Jerusalem an horrible thing: they commit adultery, and walk in lies: they strengthen also the hands of evildoers, that none doth return from his wickedness: they are all of them unto me as Sodom, and the inhabitants thereof as Gomorrah.

Now, The Most High is focusing on what the Prophets in Jerusalem are doing. They cheat on The Most High, walking in lies, saying The Most High said this, and The Most High said that, when The Most High has not spoken to them. They strengthen the hands of evildoers, like our Pastors in the church today. They know The Most High God's Law on same-sex activity.

Leviticus 18:<u>22</u> Thou shalt not lie with mankind, as with womankind: it *is* abomination.

The Pastor today know that the above precept is in the Bible, but they cancel all the Laws out except TITHING. They strengthen these gay people's hands in their congregation, putting them in charge of the Ministry of Music. The Most High consider them all part of fire and brimstone

Isaiah 5:<u>13</u> Therefore my people are gone into captivity, because *they have* no knowledge: and their honorable men *are* famished, and their multitude dried up with thirst.

Jeremiah is witnessing the Jews who are about to go into captivity. The Honorable men are the Prophets and Priests, who have no Knowledge of The Most High God, leading the Jews astray. This is the same identical path our people are taking today. You can teach according to how The Most High tells you to teach, and our people are so accustomed to hearing lies, they will not believe you and become angry with you.

Isaiah 5:<u>14</u> Therefore hell hath enlarged herself, and opened her mouth without measure: and their glory, and their multitude, and their pomp, and he that rejoiceth, shall descend into it.

Because of these Lies being taught by their Pastors, hell has gotten larger. Our people going to church on the wrong day, singing and rejoicing, being haughty (pompous), cannot tell them nothing. All the while they are descending into hell.

The BLOOD of The Covenants

Jeremiah 23:15 Therefore thus saith the LORD of hosts concerning the prophets; Behold, I will feed them with wormwood, and make them drink the water of gall: for from the prophets of Jerusalem is profaneness gone forth into all the land.

Wormwood - a state or source of bitterness or grief.

The lying Prophet were filled with grief. When the Babylonians came, I am certain they witness their families getting slaughtered before their deaths.

Gall - bold and impudent behavior.

When the Babylonians came, they did not show the Lying Prophets any respect that they thought they deserved.

Jeremiah 23:16 Thus saith the LORD of hosts, Hearken not unto the words of the prophets that prophesy unto you: they make you vain: they speak a vision of their own heart, *and* not out of the mouth of the LORD.

Do not listen to these lying Pastors and Prophets. You are living a LIE. Their visions are not according to the Law. The Most High is the GOD of Abraham, Isaac, and Jacob. His Laws represent Him. He does not go outside of Himself. That is FOOLISHNESS!

Jeremiah 23:17 They say still unto them that despise me, The LORD hath said, Ye shall have peace; and they say unto everyone that walketh after the imagination of his own heart, No evil shall come upon you.

You are acting outside of the Law, but they say that The Most High does not care, that noting bad is going to happen to you, that you cannot help who you are, or that "God hates the sin, but loves the sinner."

Jeremiah 23:20 The anger of the LORD shall not return, until he have executed, and till he have performed the thoughts of his heart: in the latter days ye shall consider it perfectly.

The Most High will not stop being angry until he does everything that He has in His mind to do to the Prophets and Priest.

The BLOOD of The Covenants

Jeremiah 23:21 I have not sent these prophets, yet they ran: I have not spoken to them, yet they prophesied.

The Most High has not sent these Lying Prophets, but they are prophesying every Sabbath and Sunday, which is the wrong day to give the Elohim of Abraham, Isaac, and Jacob praise. There are many so-called Prophets who run to the streets with the WRONG message, talking to the WRONG people and on the WRONG corners. It is evident that The Most High did not send them.

Ezekiel 3:11 And go, get thee to them of the captivity, unto the children of thy people, and speak unto them, and tell them, Thus saith the Lord GOD; whether they will hear, or whether they will forbear.

The Most High never told His Prophets to speak to the other nations, telling them their judgment when Christ comes. He told them to get to the people of the CAPTIVITY, and use His WORDS, whether they listen or do not listen.

Jeremiah 23:25 I have heard what the prophets said, that prophesy lies in my name, saying, I have dreamed, I have dreamed.

We still have prophets today claiming that The Most High God gave them a vision, but they are outside of the Law (no beard, fringes, bald heads, wrong diet, etc.). Now the Saints know that The Most High is not listening to them,

John 9:31 Now we know that God heareth not sinners: but if any man be a worshipper of God, and doeth his will, him he heareth.

However, his congregation is famished of the Law because their lying pastor does not teach them the Law. Instead, he comes out of his thoughts about visions and dreams that he claims are from The Most High God.

The BLOOD of The Covenants

Jeremiah 23:<u>26 </u>How long shall *this* be in the heart of the prophets that prophesy lies? yea, *they are* prophets of the deceit of their own heart;

The BLOOD of The Covenants

Chapter 12: The Most High Divorces the Levite Priest

When The Most High divorces the Levites, who are the Mediators that will receive the sacrifices from the Israelites for the remission of sins?

Malachi 1:6 A son honoureth *his* father, and a servant his master: if then I *be* a father, where *is* mine honor? and if I *be* a master, where *is* my fear? saith the LORD of hosts unto you, O priests, that despise my name. And ye say, Wherein have we despised thy name?

Hebrews, we have the same problem today. Many of you say that you LOVE your Mother and Father, but most of you do nothing that they tell you to do. Many of you say that you LOVE The Most High God, but you do not understand how to love Him.

1 John 5:3 For this is the love of God, that we keep his commandments: and his commandments are not grievous.

The Most High tells you how to LOVE Him, yet many of you give LIP SERVICE

Isaiah 29:13 Wherefore the Lord said, Forasmuch as this people draw near *me* with their mouth, and with their lips do honor me, but have removed their heart far from me, and their fear toward me is taught by the precept of men:

The Most High knows His children. You are so full of it! All of you have RELATIONSHIP issues. You do not know how to LOVE your GOD, nor do you know how to LOVE each other. If your Pastor does not say it, then it is not true, and many Israelites argue against the scriptures.

Malachi 1:7 Ye offer polluted bread upon mine altar; and ye say, Wherein have we polluted thee? In that ye say, The table of the LORD *is* contemptible.

The problem that The Most High had with the Levite Priest during this time was they were claiming to LOVE The Most High, but they would

The BLOOD of The Covenants

not change the Shewbread upon the Altar. When you are expecting important guest in your home, you make certain that you have FRESH bread. However, the God of Abraham, Isaac, and Jacob, you had no time to make fresh bread, and the Priest saw nothing wrong with it.

Malachi 1:8 And if ye offer the blind for sacrifice, *is it* not evil? and if ye offer the lame and sick, *is it* not evil? offer it now unto thy governor; will he be pleased with thee, or accept thy person? saith the LORD of hosts.

Another problem that The Most High had with those who were the MEDIATORS of His Covenant is they were offering LAME and SICK animals, which The Most High told them not to do in His Law. Evil is when you know it is WRONG, but do it anyway

Leviticus 22:22 Blind, or broken, or maimed, or having a wen, or scurvy, or scabbed, ye shall not offer these unto the LORD, nor make an offering by fire of them upon the altar unto the LORD.

The Levites were told not to offer blind and sick animals by fire to Him. If you had important guest, you would not cook up a lame animal and serve it to them. You will prepare the best meat that you can afford. We Hebrews need to check our ACTIONS.

1 Samuel 2:3 Talk no more so exceeding proudly; let *not* arrogancy come out of your mouth: for the LORD *is* a God of knowledge, and by him actions are weighed.

Your ACTIONS determine your LOVE for The Most High and to your Brothers and Sisters.

Malachi 1:9 And now, I pray you, beseech God that he will be gracious unto us: this hath been by your means: will he regard your persons? saith the LORD of hosts.

The BLOOD of The Covenants

The Most High will not be merciful (gracious) to you doing things by your means, and not according to the Law, as He instructed. He is not going to accept your person.

Malachi 1:10 Who *is there* even among you that would shut the doors *for nought*? neither do ye kindle *fire* on mine altar for nought. I have no pleasure in you, saith the LORD of hosts, neither will I accept an offering at your hand.

Now, The Most High asked the question: who among you Jews will go to the Temple and
SHUT the DOOR and kick the Levites out until they change their behavior. Not one Jew rose up for The Most High God. Here, The Most High **FIRED THE LEVITE PRIEST**. Since not one Jew rose up for The Most High God, guess what happened?

Since The Levites No Longer Wanted to Be Mediators to the Covenant and the Jews No Longer Wanted to Worship Their God

1 Maccabees 1:20 And after that Antiochus had smitten Egypt, he returned again in the hundred forty and third year, and went up against Israel and Jerusalem with a great multitude,

Let us establish the timeline of king Antiochus

Antiochus IV Epiphanes

Antiochus IV Epiphanes ("manifestation of the god"): name of a Seleucid king, ruled from 175 to 164 B.C.E.

• 173 or 172: visit to Jerusalem

Source: https://www.livius.org/articles/person/antiochus-iv-epiphanes/

History also reports that Antiochus entered into Jerusalem. The Most High got tired of our LIP SERVICE and bad deeds. Let us see what He did.

The BLOOD of The Covenants

1 Maccabees 1:21 And entered proudly into the sanctuary, and took away the golden altar, and the candlestick of light, and all the vessels thereof

I know Antiochus thought it was his doing, but The Most High sent Antiochus to remove His things from disobedient children,

1 Maccabees 1:22 And the table of the shewbread, and the pouring vessels, and the vials. and the censers of gold, and the veil, and the crown, and the golden ornaments that were before the temple, all which he pulled off.

Since the Levites did not want to change the Shewbread, The Most High removed the entire Shewbread table and all of His things

1 Maccabees 1:23 He took also the silver and the gold, and the precious vessels: also he took the hidden treasures which he found.

1 Maccabees 1:24 And when he had taken all away, he went into his own land, having made a great massacre, and spoken very proudly.

Not one Jew wanted to Stand up for The Most High God for the EVIL the Levites were committing. Why were the Jews upset when Antiochus was removing The Most High God's things? They took The Most High for granted and many lost their lives protesting against His removal from them.

1 Maccabees 1:41 Moreover king Antiochus wrote to his whole kingdom, that all should be one people,

The Most High God did not want the Jews even worshiping Him. Being "One People" simply meant that the Jews could no longer be HOLY.

1 Maccabees 1:42 And every one should leave his laws: so all the heathen agreed according to the commandment of the king.

The BLOOD of The Covenants

The Most High was not forgiving you for a lame and blind sacrifice. You may as well leave your Laws because you were not being forgiven with a Lame sacrifice and dirty Shewbread on the Altar.

1 Maccabees 1:43 Yea, many also of the Israelites consented to his religion, and sacrificed unto idols, and profaned the sabbath.

Many of us were WICKED already, not wanting to keep the Laws, Statues and Commandments. This is the same Spirit among the Hebrews today. We will do anything EXCEPT what The Most High God instructed us to do.

1 Maccabees 1:44 For the king had sent letters by messengers unto Jerusalem and the cities of Juda that they should follow the strange laws of the land,

The King made certain that the Jews followed these new Laws.

1 Maccabees 1:45 And forbid burnt offerings, and sacrifice, and drink offerings, in the temple; and that they should profane the sabbaths and festival days:

This was our punishment, because the Levites did not want to be in SERVICE to The Most High God on behalf of the Jews and none in Jerusalem stood up.

1 Maccabees 1:46 And pollute the sanctuary and holy people:

1 Maccabees 1:48 That they should also leave their children uncircumcised, and make their souls abominable with all manner of uncleanness and profanation:

Esau's methods of accomplishing the above have changed, yet the results are EXACTLY the SAME. All of that pork, shellfish and catfish is sold in Hebrew communities. Most of the children are born out of wedlock and the LAWLESSNESS in ALL of our communities.

The BLOOD of The Covenants

1 Maccabees 1:<u>49</u> To the end they might forget the law, and change all the ordinances.

Their intentions were to make us FORGET The Most High God's Laws, Statues and Commandments. They succeeded!

1 Maccabees 1:<u>50</u> And whosoever would not do according to the commandment of the king, he said, he should die.

It is on AUTOMATIC now. We Hebrews have been programmed to defile ourselves.

The Levites Had Departed From the Law

Malachi 2:<u>4</u> And ye shall know that I have sent this commandment unto you, that my covenant might be with Levi, saith the LORD of hosts.

The Levites were in services to The Most High God. They were the tribe that made daily sacrifices, took care of the Temple, and made sacrifices for the people

Deuteronomy 10:<u>8</u> At that time the LORD separated the tribe of Levi, to bear the ark of the covenant of the LORD, to stand before the LORD to minister unto him, and to bless in his name, unto this day.

The Covenant was with Levi, they were the administrators

Malachi 2:<u>5</u> My covenant was with him of life and peace; and I gave them to him *for* the fear wherewith he feared me, and was afraid before my name.

This was how Levi was in the beginning. They feared The Most High God's judgments.

Malachi 2:<u>6</u> The law of truth was in his mouth, and iniquity was not found in his lips: he walked with me in peace and equity, and did turn many away from iniquity.

The BLOOD of The Covenants

The Levites administered the Law and there was no sin found with them. They walked with The Most High God and turned many of our people away from SIN.

Malachi 2:7 For the priest's lips should keep knowledge, and they should seek the law at his mouth: for he *is* the messenger of the LORD of hosts.

If you are claiming to be in SERVICE to The Most High God calling yourself a Minister, Pastor, Reverend, Bishop, etc. the knowledge that you are supposed to keep is the Laws of The Most High God. Your congregation should be seeking the Laws at your mouth.

Malachi 2:8 But ye are departed out of the way; ye have caused many to stumble at the law; ye have corrupted the covenant of Levi, saith the LORD of hosts.

The tribe of Levi forgot who Our GOD was. They departed from the Commandments. How can they serve The Most High when they made themselves unclean?

Leviticus 11:45 For I *am* the LORD that bringeth you up out of the land of Egypt, to be your God: ye shall therefore be holy, for I *am* holy.

The Levites made themselves unclean, unfit to be in the SERVICE to The Most High God. How did The Most High punish them as a tribe?

Malachi 2:9 Therefore have I also made you contemptible and base before all the people, according as ye have not kept my ways, but have been partial in the law.

The present-day Levites are despised and are at the BOTTOM, among ALL of the twelve tribes. We are at the BOTTOM of society, but the tribe of Levi will be even LOWER. Many believe that these are the Haitians today.

The BLOOD of The Covenants

The Coming of Christ

Malachi 3:1 Behold, I will send my messenger, and he shall prepare the way before me: and the Lord, whom ye seek, shall suddenly come to his temple, even the messenger of the covenant, whom ye delight in: behold, he shall come, saith the LORD of hosts.

What Messenger was sent?

Matthew 11:7 And as they departed, Jesus began to say unto the multitudes concerning John, What went ye out into the wilderness to see? A reed shaken with the wind?

The Messiah was referring to **John the Baptist**. They asked the Jews what type of man were they expecting to see, a weakened scary man?

Matthew 11:8 But what went ye out for to see? A man clothed in soft raiment? behold, they that wear soft *clothing* are in kings' houses.

Neither did you see a man in fine garments from the king's house

Matthew 11:9 But what went ye out for to see? A prophet? yea, I say unto you, and more than a prophet.

John the Baptist was more than a Prophet

Matthew 11:10 For this is *he*, of whom it is written, Behold, I send my messenger before thy face, which shall prepare thy way before thee.

John the Baptist was sent to the Israelites to prepare them for Christ.

Malachi 3:2 But who may abide the day of his coming? and who shall stand when he appeareth? for he *is* like a refiner's fire, and like fullers' soap:

Here it is referring to the Messiah's second coming, when He returns as a GOD! Who will be able to abide during this time?

The BLOOD of The Covenants

Revelation 22:<u>14</u> Blessed *are* they that do his commandments, that they may have right to the tree of life, and may enter in through the gates into the city.

Malachi 3:<u>3</u> And he shall sit *as* a refiner and purifier of silver: and he shall purify the sons of Levi, and purge them as gold and silver, that they may offer unto the LORD an offering in righteousness.

There will be some Levites in the one-third. that will be saved

Zechariah 13:<u>9</u> And I will bring the third part through the fire, and will refine them as silver is refined, and will try them as gold is tried: they shall call on my name, and I will hear them: I will say, It *is* my people: and they shall say, The LORD *is* my God.

Christ will refine the one-third, removing the impurities from us. All of the RIGHTEOUS are struggling with something. These impurities will be removed from us.

Malachi 3:<u>4</u> Then shall the offering of Judah and Jerusalem be pleasant unto the LORD, as in the days of old, and as in former years.

When the Southern Kingdom is purified, then our offerings will be pleasing to The Most High.

Malachi 3:<u>6</u> For I *am* the LORD, I change not; therefore ye sons of Jacob are not consumed.

The Most High God will not abandon His people. Although He is punishing His people, there is an end to our punishment.

The Deception of Tithing

Malachi 3:<u>8</u> Will a man rob God? Yet ye have robbed me. But ye say, Wherein have we robbed thee? In tithes and offerings.

This is the precept that many Christian Ministers uses, leading their parishioners to believe that you are robbing The Most High when you do not give 10% of your money, even before you pay your debts. Let us understand **What is TITHES?**

Deuteronomy 14:<u>22</u> Thou shalt truly tithe all the increase of thy seed, that the field bringeth forth year by year.

TITHES were CROPS not MONEY

Deuteronomy 14:<u>23</u> And thou shalt eat before the LORD thy God, in the place which he shall choose to place his name there, the tithe of thy corn, of thy wine, and of thine oil, and the firstlings of thy herds and of thy flocks; that thou mayest learn to fear the LORD thy God always.

TITHES were also CORN, WINE, OIL, HERDS, and FLOCKS

Why were the Israelites instructed to pay TITHES?

Deuteronomy 14:<u>29</u> And the Levite, (because he hath no part nor inheritance with thee,) and the stranger, and the fatherless, and the widow, which *are* within thy gates, shall come, and shall eat and be satisfied; that the LORD thy God may bless thee in all the work of thine hand which thou doest.

TITHES were for the Levites, Hebrews visiting, the fatherless, and widows. Tithes was never money for the Preacher.

Malachi 3:<u>9</u> Ye *are* cursed with a curse: for ye have robbed me, *even* this whole nation.

Now you should understand why The Most High is upset. The HAVES are not taking care of the HAVE NOTS.

The Most High Will Open the Windows of Heaven

Malachi 3:<u>10</u> Bring ye all the tithes into the storehouse, that there may be meat in mine house, and prove me now herewith, saith the LORD of hosts, if I will not open you the windows of heaven, and pour you out a blessing, that *there shall* not *be room* enough *to receive it.*

The BLOOD of The Covenants

You do not store MONEY in a STOREHOUSE. There was no food in the STOREHOUSES for the Levites, fatherless, widows and strangers. Many of you think that The Most High will open a **window of heaven and pour out blessings**. That is not what this means. Let us understand **what the windows of heaven.**

Genesis 7:11 In the six hundredth year of Noah's life, in the second month, the seventeenth day of the month, the same day were all the fountains of the great deep broken up, and the windows of heaven were opened.

The **Windows of heaven** were opened. What happened when they opened?

Genesis 7:12 And the rain was upon the earth forty days and forty nights.

Rain fell upon the Earth! The Most High was saying that he would open the windows of heaven and rain will fall upon your fields and bless you with an increase in your crops.

Malachi 3:11 And I will rebuke the devourer for your sakes, and he shall not destroy the fruits of your ground; neither shall your vine cast her fruit before the time in the field, saith the LORD of hosts.

The Most High will also keep away the locust, grasshoppers, worms that devour your crops

Malachi 3:12 And all nations shall call you blessed: for ye shall be a delightsome land, saith the LORD of hosts.

This is written in the Law of Moses

Deuteronomy 4:5 Behold, I have taught you statutes and judgments, even as the LORD my God commanded me, that ye should do so in the land whither ye go to possess it.

The BLOOD of The Covenants

Moses taught the Israelites Laws, Statues and Judgments as he was commanded by The Most High God.

Deuteronomy 4:6 Keep therefore and do *them*; for this *is* your wisdom and your understanding in the sight of the nations, which shall hear all these statutes, and say, Surely this great nation *is* a wise and understanding people.

We are instructed to keep the Commandments and do them. This is how the other nations know that we have WISDOM and UNDERSTANDING. Because we do not keep the Commandments, no nations see the Israelites as wise or understanding. You can look at our communities and see that we are LAWLESS

The Most High Wants His Chosen to Understand How It Feels When Someone Cheat On You.

We have been taking Our God for granted for so long that He told Hosea the Prophet to find a wife who is in love with another, and see how it feels when she cheats with another.

Hosea 3:1 Then said the LORD unto me, Go yet, love a woman beloved of *her* friend, yet an adulteress, according to the love of the LORD toward the children of Israel, who look to other gods, and love flagons of wine.

The Most High told the Prophet Hosea to go Love a woman, who is an adulteress according to the Commandments (Love) of GOD..

Leviticus 18:20 Moreover thou shalt not lie carnally with thy neighbor's wife, to defile thyself with her.

Adultery, according to The Most High God's Law is physically laying with another man's wife, or another woman's husband.

Leviticus 20:10 And the man that committeth adultery with *another* man's wife, *even he* that committeth adultery with his neighbor's wife, the adulterer and the adulteress shall surely be put to death.

The BLOOD of The Covenants

Having a physical relationship with someone that belongs to another, there is a label for that.

Hosea 3:2 So I bought her to me for fifteen *pieces* of silver, and *for* an homer of barley, and an half homer of barley:

The Bible teaches us things that we have lost over the years. The Hebrew culture required that a man had to pay something for a wife. Hosea negotiated fifteen pieces of silver and approximately seventy ounces (homer and a half) of barley.

Hosea 3:3 And I said unto her, Thou shalt abide for me many days; thou shalt not play the harlot, and thou shalt not be for *another* man: so *will* I also *be* for thee.

Hosea gave his wife HIS LAWS, the same way that The Most High gave His wife (Israel) the Laws. Hosea told her that she will be with him forever, that she does not sleep around with other men, that she will only be for him. The Most High God also chose the Israelites to Himself.

Exodus 19:5 Now therefore, if ye will obey my voice indeed, and keep my covenant, then ye shall be a peculiar treasure unto me above all people: for all the earth *is* mine:

When the Israelites are OBEDIENT to Their GOD, we are SPECIAL or PARTICULAR to Him. This makes it impossible to Love The Most High God of Abraham, Isaac, and Jacob and the world at the same time.

Hosea 3:4 For the children of Israel shall abide many days without a king, and without a prince, and without a sacrifice, and without an image, and without an ephod, and *without* teraphim:

This chapter is an allegory or metaphor that shows a man marrying an adulterous woman and she is cheating on him with many lovers, the same way that the children of Israel are cheating on their GOD with many gods, when He only gave the Israelites, His wife, the RULES to be in His House.

The BLOOD of The Covenants

Jeremiah 3:14 Turn, O backsliding children, saith the LORD; for I am married unto you: and I will take you one of a city, and two of a family, and I will bring you to Zion:

In this society, the Israelites have lost a lot of knowledge. Every Husband has LAWS, or RULES for his family, and they do not apply to those who are not under his roof., unless he has authority over them. The RULES of Our God does not apply to the other nations, only to His people.

Hosea 3:5 Afterward shall the children of Israel return, and seek the LORD their God, and David their king; and shall fear the LORD and his goodness in the latter days.

After some events occurred, the children of Israel shall return to The Most High God.

Amos 3:1 Hear this word that the LORD hath spoken against you, O children of Israel, against the whole family which I brought up from the land of Egypt, saying,

The God of this Bible is exclusive only to the Israelites.

Amos 3:2 You only have I known of all the families of the earth: therefore I will punish you for all your iniquities.

This is an EXCLUSIVE statement and The Most High only punishes those that He gave His RULES to be in His House, the people that He made a Blood Covenant..

The BLOOD of The Covenants

Chapter 13: Many Generations Had Passed From Abraham to Christ.

The Israelites have rebelled against their God. First, He split the kingdom after King Solomon rebelled against him. Jeroboam took ten tribes, which included portion of the Levites, who were in every city. These ten tribes go by the name of Israel, the Northern Kingdom, Ephraim, or is referred to as Samaria. The two tribes that The Most High allowed Rehoboam, the son of Solomon to keep, were two tribes, three with a portion of the Levites. These three tribes were called Judah, the Southern Kingdom, or is referred to as Jerusalem.

Matthew 1:17 So all the generations from Abraham to David *are* fourteen generations; and from David until the carrying away into Babylon *are* fourteen generations; and from the carrying away into Babylon unto Christ *are* fourteen generations.

How Long is Fourteen Generations?
Is fourteen generation the same throughout the ages?

Source: https://www.bibleversestudy.com/matthew/matthew1-14-generations.htm

What is meant by "generations" in the passage above?
God renamed Abram, who was born in 2167 BC, "Abraham" in 2068 BC when he was "ninety-nine years old" (Genesis 17:1); David was crowned king in 1010 BC; the southern kingdom of Judah was deported to Babylon in 586 BC; and Jesus was born about 6 BC (see When was Jesus born?). This means that the first set of "fourteen generations" in Matthew 1:17 covered 1,058 years (2068 BC to 1010 BC), the second set of "fourteen generations" covered 424 years (1010 BC to 586 BC), and the third set of "fourteen generations" covered about 580 years (586 BC to 6 BC). So, these were not fourteen directly sequential generations.

A New Blood Covenant Is Required
After The Most High God fired the Levites, a NEW BLOOD Covenant is required, not to include the Whole World, but to place those who was under the original Covenant under a NEW Covenant. Blood was required for the OLD Covenant, with the Levites as the

The BLOOD of The Covenants

Mediators, and BLOOD is required for the NEW Covenant, with Christ as the MEDIATOR and the New High Priest.,

Hebrews 9:11 But Christ being come an high priest of good things to come, by a greater and more perfect tabernacle, not made with hands, that is to say, not of this building;

When Christ was born, He knew that He would be the sacrifice to re-establish the Covenant with our GOD. This Covenant was not only for the Jews but also for Samaria, or the Northern Kingdom, who The Most High God had divorced.

Jeremiah 3:8 And I saw, when for all the causes whereby backsliding Israel committed adultery I had put her away, and given her a bill of divorce; yet her treacherous sister Judah feared not, but went and played the harlot also.

Let me remind you that the Jews, short for JUDAH, consisted of three tribes, Judah, Benjamin, and partial tribe of Levi. Christ came to die for ALL TWELVE TRIBES. Only His Disciples understood this. Furthermore, when Christ came, He did not come to uphold the Tabernacle dealing with the Old Covenant, because His Father's Spirit was long departed.

Hebrews 9:12 Neither by the blood of goats and calves, but by his own blood he entered in once into the holy place, having obtained eternal redemption *for us*.

Animal sacrifices dealing with the OLD Covenant was no longer acceptable, nor the Levite Priest who sacrificed them. Imagine this, the Levites were so accustomed to being taken care of, that they did not want to abolish this system. Remember, the sacrifice that was burned or cooked on the altar, the Levite men ate, along with the shoulder and other parts of the animal. The Most High no longer accepted animal sacrifices, and Christ being the New High Priest, His Tabernacle is created in Heaven.

The BLOOD of The Covenants

Hebrews 9:13 For if the blood of bulls and of goats, and the ashes of an heifer sprinkling the unclean, sanctifieth to the purifying of the flesh:

This is discussing how an Israelite was purified and cleansed of SIN using the BLOOD of bulls, sheep and goats and sprinkling them with ashes, under the Old Covenant.

Hebrews 9:14 How much more shall the blood of Christ, who through the eternal Spirit offered himself without spot to God, purge your conscience from dead works to serve the living God?

The BLOOD of animals could not cleanse an Israelite from all SINS,. However, the BLOOD of Christ can cleanse you from ALL sins, except lying against the Holy Ghost.

How Do You Speak Against the Holy Ghost?
You must first understand who receives the Holy Ghost, because everyone does not receive it. Even though they are going to church on Sunday, the Holy Ghost is not in them.

Matthew 12:32 And whosoever speaketh a word against the Son of man, it shall be forgiven him: but whosoever speaketh against the Holy Ghost, it shall not be forgiven him, neither in this world, neither in the *world* to come.

Before you can receive the Holy Ghost, you must Believe in Christ according to the Scriptures, not according to your Pastor or denomination.

John 7:38 He that believeth on me, as the scripture hath said, out of his belly shall flow rivers of living water.

This "**river of living water**" is referring to the Holy Ghost, but the stipulation is that you must believe on Christ as the scripture says.

John 7:39 (But this spake he of the Spirit, which they that believe on him should receive: for the Holy Ghost was not yet *given*; because that Jesus was not yet glorified.)

The BLOOD of The Covenants

Christ was speaking of the Holy Ghost before He died and arose again, before He was taken up.

John 14:26 But the Comforter, *which is* the Holy Ghost, whom the Father will send in my name, he shall teach you all things, and bring all things to your remembrance, whatsoever I have said unto you.

Everyone who claims to have the Holy Ghost have never received the Holy Ghost, because they do not believe in Christ according to the SCRIPTURES. Just because they are shouting on Sunday, does not mean they have the Holy Ghost. Just because many Israelites are in these Hebrew camps, the same way the Jews were gathering in Jerusalem during the time of Christ, it does not mean they have the Holy Ghost.

In order for an Israelite to speak against the Holy Ghost means he or she once believed in Christ as the scriptures has said.

Hebrews 6:4 For *it is* impossible for those who were once enlightened, and have tasted of the heavenly gift, and were made partakers of the Holy Ghost,

The only way that an Israelite can receive the Holy Ghost and become enlightened is you MUST believe in Christ according to the scriptures, and you have learned RIGHTEOUSNESS and about the Kingdom of Heaven.

Hebrews 6:5 And have tasted the good word of God, and the powers of the world to come,

When an Israelite receives the Holy Ghost, he or she have tasted the word of GOD, and understand the world that is coming.

Hebrews 6:6 If they shall fall away, to renew them again unto repentance; seeing they crucify to themselves the Son of God afresh, and put *him* to an open shame.

There is nothing out there in these streets! Yet, many Israelites backslide back into the WORLD after receiving the Holy Ghost.

The BLOOD of The Covenants

When an Israelite does this, he or she has done two things: 1) you have crucified Christ again, because His BLOOD had already washed you clean, and 2) you are endangering yourself of hellfire and being REMOVED from the Book of Life

Hebrews 9:15 And for this cause he is the mediator of the new testament, that by means of death, for the redemption of the transgressions *that were* under the first testament, they which are called might receive the promise of eternal inheritance.

Christ is the MEDIATOR of the NEW Covenant, who goes to the Father on the Israelites' behalf. This is in comparison to the Levites who offered up sacrifices for the forgiveness of SIN on the Israelites' behalf. Christ died for the Israelites' sake. His BLOOD was similar in comparison to the blood of the oxen that Moses collected in large basins for the Covenant that The Most High God made..

John 1:35 Again the next day after John stood, and two of his disciples;

John the Baptist, along with two Disciples who saw Christ, whom John the Baptist never met.

John 1:36 And looking upon Jesus as he walked, he saith, Behold the Lamb of God!

However, John the Baptist saw Christ and immediately knew that He was the Lamb of God, who will be sacrificed for His People.

Hebrews 9:16 For where a testament *is*, there must also of necessity be the death of the testator.

The New Testament did not take effect until Christ died.

The Purpose of the Death of Christ
Many people think that Christ died for the benefit of the entire world. You are being sold a huge LIE!

The BLOOD of The Covenants

Romans 9:3 For I could wish that myself were accursed from Christ for my brethren, my kinsmen according to the flesh:

Apostle Paul is saying that he wished that he could have gone through the same tragedy as Christ for his BROTHERS, according to the flesh. This is not according to the SPIRIT, but according to the descendants of Abraham, Isaac, and Jacob.

Romans 9:4 Who are Israelites; to whom *pertaineth* the adoption, and the glory, and the covenants, and the giving of the law, and the service *of God*, and the promises;

The descendants of Jacob are called Israelites. Why?

Genesis 32:28 And he said, Thy name shall be called no more Jacob, but Israel: for as a prince hast thou power with God and with men, and hast prevailed.

Israel means a PRINCE that has POWER with The Most High God and with men and has prevailed

Christ died for the Israelites, the descendants of Jacob. His Blood adopted all of us back to the fold, especially the Northern Kingdom. Everything that Christ did was for the Israelites.

Romans 9:5 Whose *are* the fathers, and of whom as concerning the flesh Christ *came*, who is over all, God blessed forever. Amen.

Christ came and died for the descendants of Jacob.

Hebrews 2:8 Thou hast put all things in subjection under his feet. For in that he put all in subjection under him, he left nothing *that is* not put under him. But now we see not yet all things put under him.

The death of Christ was done to re-organize the nation of Israel under His charge. The nation of Israel has to go to Him for forgiveness of SINS. He is also the New High Priest who sits at the right hand of GOD.

The BLOOD of The Covenants

Romans 8:34 Who *is* he that condemneth? *It is* Christ that died, yea rather, that is risen again, who is even at the right hand of God, who also maketh intercession for us.

Christ is sitting at the right hand of God on the behalf of His people according to the FLESH, who are Israelites! In the Old Covenant, the blood of animals could not REDEEM an Israelite when he violated the Sabbath, commit adultery, bestiality, etc. However, with the BLOOD of Christ, you can be forgiven from all of these Sins. If you continue to do these sins and run to Christ for forgiveness, then there is no more forgiveness for you. The well will run dry!

Hebrew 10:26 For if we sin willfully after that we have received the knowledge of the truth, there remaineth no more sacrifice for sins,

The Blood of Christ is not to be used for an Israelite to willfully SIN, knowing that it is wrong, then ask for forgiveness, and he continues to do the same sin and ask for forgiveness over and over again. Christ does not want Israelites using His Blood to help them in their wickedness.

Hebrews 2:14 Forasmuch then as the children are partakers of flesh and blood, he also himself likewise took part of the same; that through death he might destroy him that had the power of death, that is, the devil;

Christ did not come down as an Angel, but as a man, the same flesh as the children of Israel, to destroy the devil through His death. The devil has no power over Israelites in death because of Christ. Because the Levites had been FIRED, there were no MEDIATORS for nearly five hundred years, and if you committed any sin, the blood of animals would not cover you.

Hebrews 2:16 For verily he took not on *him the nature of* angels; but he took on *him* the seed of Abraham.

It is especially important to understand that Christ was born of the SEED of Abraham, Isaac, and Jacob. He did not come as a CELESTIAL being.

The BLOOD of The Covenants

Hebrews 2:17 Wherefore in all things it behoved him to be made like unto *his* brethren, that he might be a merciful and faithful high priest in things *pertaining* to God, to make reconciliation for the sins of the people.

Christ made the decision to be like the Israelites, His Brothers, so that He can understand what their day-to-day struggles were, their lust and temptations. As an Angel, Christ would not have this Israelite experience. It is RIGHT and WRONG with them.

Hebrews 2:18 For in that he himself hath suffered being tempted, he is able to succor them that are tempted.

Because Christ was being tempted, He was able to show His Disciples how to avoid temptation and sin

1 Corinthians 6:18 Flee fornication. Every sin that a man doeth is without the body; but he that committeth fornication sinneth against his own body.

Christ taught Israelites how to avoid Temptation, knowing that EVERY sin that an Israelite does in OUTSIDE of the body, meaning that an Israelite is committing transgression AGAINST his BROTHER or SISTER. There are many things that many of you camps call SIN which does not qualify.

1 Corinthians 6:19 What? know ye not that your body is the temple of the Holy Ghost *which is* in you, which ye have of God, and ye are not your own?

An Israelite's BODY, who has FAITH in Christ AND is keeping the Commandments of The Most High God, is the temple of the Holy Ghost. Knowing that SIN occurs OUTSIDE the body then HOW do you defile your temple?

Romans 6:23 For the wages of sin *is* death; but the gift of God *is* eternal life through Jesus Christ our Lord.

SIN is how an Israelite DEFILES his Temple.

The BLOOD of The Covenants

1 Corinthians 6:20 For ye are bought with a price: therefore glorify God in your body, and in your spirit, which are God's.

Christ purchased the Israelites back by sacrificing His LIFE, and the Israelites are supposed to worship The Most High God by keeping His Laws, Statues and Commandments.

Hebrews 9:17 For a testament *is* of force after men are dead: otherwise it is of no strength at all while the testator liveth.

I can write a WILL or TESTAMENT, but it has no POWER, or the WILL cannot be executed until after I die. This is the same as Christ, who knew that He came to be betrayed and die at the hand of the Romans who, pursued Him from birth, and His own people.

Mark 9:31 For he taught his disciples, and said unto them, The Son of man is delivered into the hands of men, and they shall kill him; and after that he is killed, he shall rise the third day.

Imagine knowing all the particulars of your death, your purpose? That is hard to imagine.

Hebrews 9:18 Whereupon neither the first *testament* was dedicated without blood.

Both Covenants, Old Testament, and the New Testament, required BLOOD.

Hebrews 9:19 For when Moses had spoken every precept to all the people according to the law, he took the blood of calves and of goats, with water, and scarlet wool, and hyssop, and sprinkled both the book, and all the people,

The hyssop is from the mint family, and Moses used it to neutralize the smell of the blood that was sprinkled on everything, including The Most High God's people.

Hebrews 9:20 Saying, This *is* the blood of the testament which God hath enjoined unto you.

The BLOOD of The Covenants

Under the Old Covenant, the Israelites were covered in animal BLOOD, but under the New Covenant, the Israelites are covered under the BLOOD of Christ.

Hebrews 9:21 Moreover he sprinkled with blood both the tabernacle, and all the vessels of the ministry.

Under the Old Covenant, everything was covered in BLOOD.

Hebrews 9:22 And almost all things are by the law purged with blood; and without shedding of blood is no remission.

Blood is involved for the remission of SINS. Christ shed His Blood once and He is the New High Priest that sits at the RIGHT HAND of The Most High God interceding on the behalf of the Israelites, so that they can enter the kingdom of Heaven.

Matthew 5:48 Be ye therefore perfect, even as your Father which is in heaven is perfect.

There is no PERFECTION without the BLOOD of Christ. There are only a few Israelite who walked upon this Earth can claim to be Perfect. As for the majority of the Israelites, we are riddled in sin, because our Heritage has been stolen from us.

Jeremiah 17:4 And thou, even thyself, shalt discontinue from thine heritage that I gave thee; and I will cause thee to serve thine enemies in the land which thou knowest not: for ye have kindled a fire in mine anger, *which* shall burn forever.

An Israelite who has been mis-guided, lost to himself/herself, do not know their God, or His REQUIREMENTS, will need the BLOOD of Christ in order to become PERFECT. Without Christ's BLOOD, you are condemned, because there would be no remission for SIN.

Hebrews 9:23 *It was* therefore necessary that the patterns of things in the heavens should be purified with these; but the heavenly things themselves with better sacrifices than these.

The BLOOD of The Covenants

The "PATTERN of things" is referring to the BLOOD sacrifices of lamb, goats, and oxen, etc. However, there is a better sacrifice made in the Heavenly realm, which was Christ.

Hebrews 9:24 For Christ is not entered into the holy places made with hands, *which are* the figures of the true; but into heaven itself, now to appear in the presence of God for us:

Christ continues to go to the Father to intercede on the behalf of those who have REPENTED and RETURNED to the FOLD. He does not go to the Father on a sinner's behalf who continues to sin.

John 9:31 Now we know that God heareth not sinners: but if any man be a worshipper of God, and doeth his will, him he heareth.

Why would Christ waste His time going to the Father, when the Father does not hear you?

Hebrews 9:25 Nor yet that he should offer himself often, as the high priest entereth into the holy place every year with blood of others;

Under the New Covenant, Christ does not offer His BLOOD yearly, as the High Priest under the Old Covenant, who would go beyond the vail and offer BLOOD.

Hebrews 9:28 So Christ was once offered to bear the sins of many; and unto them that look for him shall he appear the second time without sin unto salvation.

Christ did not bear the SIN for everybody, but MANY, who are the Israelites. The Israelites are the only group that can break the Covenant of The Most High God, because He ONLY knows them and punishes them for their iniquities.

The BLOOD of The Covenants

Chapter 14: A New Covenant Was Made With the Twelve Tribes of Israel

Forget what you have been taught in these Christian Churches and in some of these Hebrew camps, what does the SCRIPTURES say?

Hebrews 8:6 But now hath he obtained a more excellent ministry, by how much also he is the mediator of a better covenant, which was established upon better promises.

Christ was an Excellent Minister. He came to SERVE, not to be served. Not only will the New Covenant be better, so will be His Kingdom to come.

Matthew 20:27 And whosoever will be chief among you, let him be your servant:

It seems that the majority of Israelites who become MINISTERS always come to be SERVED, not to serve.

Matthew 20:28 Even as the Son of man came not to be ministered unto, but to minister, and to give his life a ransom for many.

Christ obtained an excellent ministry. He did not come for people to serve Him. Not only did Christ came to SERVE, but He also came and died for the Israelites' sake.

Hebrews 8:7 For if that first *covenant* had been faultless, then should no place have been sought for the second.

The Old Covenant had many faults. The Levites, the Mediators of the Old Covenant showed no honor to The Most High God. Not only did they violate His Laws, but they also defiled His Holy Sanctuary by sacrificing lame, sick, animals with scurvy and maim.

Hebrews 8:8 For finding fault with them, he saith, Behold, the days come, saith the Lord, when I will make a new covenant with the house of Israel and with the house of Judah:

The BLOOD of The Covenants

The Israelites had messed up the Covenant so bad, that The Most High detached Himself from us to prevent us from defiling Him. This is in the New Covenant. The Most High God of Abraham, Isaac, and Jacob will make a NEW COVENANT with the TWELVE TRIBES OF ISRAEL. Regardless of what you have been taught, Christ dying on the Cross, He did not die for the WORLD.

John 17:9 I pray for them: I pray not for the world, but for them which thou hast given me; for they are thine.

Christ went to areas where the Jews lived. He did not go to the Arabs, East Indians, Chinese, Japanese, or the White, even though they were in the Land. He spoke to His People.

John 17:10 And all mine are thine, and thine are mine; and I am glorified in them.

The Most High God only sent Christ to the Israelites.

John 4:22 Ye worship ye know not what: we know what we worship: for salvation is of the Jews.

Before Christ died, He came to save the Jews first. Salvation was only for them. However, after Christ died, Salvation was extended to the Northern Kingdom, because they were divorced by The Most High God and were considered GENTILES, because they were no longer The Most High God's people. Blood was required to bring the Northern Kingdom back into the fold.

When Christ Was Alive, He Did Not Send His Disciples to Samaria?

It is important to understand, that Christ initially sent His Disciples out only to the Jews, because His BLOOD was required to bring the Samaritans back into the fold.

Matthew 10:5 These twelve Jesus sent forth, and commanded them, saying, Go not into the way of the Gentiles, and into *any* city of the Samaritans enter ye not:

The BLOOD of The Covenants

Christ specifically told His Disciples not to go to ANY Gentiles, even the Samaritans. I will show you how His instructions changed after Christ died.

Matthew 10:6 But go rather to the lost sheep of the house of Israel.

At this time, the Disciples were instructed to go only to the Jews, or the LOST SHEEP, who, by the majority, are still LOST, because they REJECTED Christ.

Matthew 10:7 And as ye go, preach, saying, The kingdom of heaven is at hand.

Christ instructed them to go to His people and preach the KINGDOM to come.

2 Esdras 6:9 For Esau is the end of the world, and Jacob is the beginning of it that followeth.

Teach them about the Kingdom after Esau's rule is over, and who it includes?

Revelation 21:12 And had a wall great and high, *and* had twelve gates, and at the gates twelve angels, and names written thereon, which are *the names* of the twelve tribes of the children of Israel:

The descendants of Jacob, all twelve tribes, are eligible for membership to the kingdom to come. However, only a portion, less than half will qualify.

Zechariah 13:8 And it shall come to pass, *that* in all the land, saith the LORD, two parts therein shall be cut off *and* die; but the third shall be left therein.

Only one-third of the twelve tribes of Israel will be eligible to enter in gates into the city. There is a requirement to get into the CITY.

The BLOOD of The Covenants

Revelation 22:14 Blessed *are* they that do his commandments, that they may have right to the tree of life, and may enter in through the gates into the city.

Christ did not FREE YOU from keeping His Father's Laws and Commandments. He came as a MEDIATOR and a SACRIFICE. When you break His Father's Laws, He sits on the RIGHT HAND of The Most High God, asking Him for forgiveness on your behalf, using His BLOOD for the remission of your SINS.

After Christ Died His Instructions Changed to Adopt the Samarians.

When Christ arose from the dead, He gave His Disciples and Believers instructions so that they could receive the Holy Ghost, and who they were instructed to Minister. Apostle Paul was given similar instructions.

Acts 1:2 Until the day in which he was taken up, after that he through the Holy Ghost had given commandments unto the apostles whom he had chosen:

When Christ died and afterwards, until He went up into Heaven, Christ spoke to His Disciples or Apostles through the Holy Ghost. They had already received the Holy Ghost when Christ sent them out.

Acts 1:3 To whom also he shewed himself alive after his passion by many infallible proofs, being seen of them forty days, and speaking of the things pertaining to the kingdom of God:

Many people saw Christ after His death, and He was seen forty days, and He was teaching the same thing that He instructed His Disciples to teach.

Acts 1:4 And, being assembled together with *them*, commanded them that they should not depart from Jerusalem, but wait for the promise of the Father, which, *saith he*, ye have heard of me.

The BLOOD of The Covenants

When Christ gathered with His Disciples and Followers, He INSTRUCTED them not to leave Jerusalem, in order to receive the Holy Ghost, the promise of The Most High God.

Acts 1:6 When they therefore were come together, they asked of him, saying, Lord, wilt thou at this time restore again the kingdom to Israel?

The Disciples and Followers asked Christ if He was coming to RESTORE the Kingdom back to the Twelve Tribes of Israel. These Jews knew that SALVATION is also for the Northern Kingdom, because they did not ask Christ if He was restoring the Kingdom back to the Jews.

Acts 1:7 And he said unto them, It is not for you to know the times or the seasons, which the Father hath put in his own power.

Nobody Knows the Day Or Time When Esau's World Ends

The Disciples wanted to know when Esau's World will end. This is part of Kingdom teaching.

Matthew 24:36 But of that day and hour knoweth no *man*, no, not the angels of heaven, but my Father only.

The Most High has not revealed the END of Esau's World, not even to the Angels.

Matthew 24:37 But as the days of Noah *were*, so shall also the coming of the Son of man be.

It is going to be the same situation when the first time the world was destroyed by water. When The Most High gives Christ the authority and DOMINION, then Jacob will be the beginning.

Daniel 7:13 I saw in the night visions, and, behold, *one* like the Son of man came with the clouds of heaven, and came to the Ancient of days, and they brought him near before him.

The Prophet Daniel saw at night the Angels leading Christ to the Throne of The Most High God

126

The BLOOD of The Covenants

Daniel 7:14 And there was given him dominion, and glory, and a kingdom, that all people, nations, and languages, should serve him: his dominion *is* an everlasting dominion, which shall not pass away, and his kingdom *that* which shall not be destroyed.

When The Most High gives Christ permission, He will also give Him POWER to rule the entire world!

Matthew 24:38 For as in the days that were before the flood they were eating and drinking, marrying and giving in marriage, until the day that Noe entered into the ark,

When Christ comes, everybody will be living their BEST LIFE, and when they see the destruction, they will be overcome with EXTREME FEAR.

Isaiah 13:6 Howl ye; for the day of the LORD *is* at hand; it shall come as a destruction from the Almighty.

When Christ returns, everybody will be partying, getting married, having children out of wedlock, baby daddy, and baby momma drama, and this destruction will come without warning.

Isaiah 13:7 Therefore shall all hands be faint, and every man's heart shall melt:

Then, everyone will be scared, so nervous, that they will not be able to do anything, because of the fear.

Isaiah 13:8 And they shall be afraid: pangs and sorrows shall take hold of them; they shall be in pain as a woman that travaileth: they shall be amazed one at another; their faces *shall be as* flames.

Do not think that you have plenty of time to get RIGHT with The Most High God.

Ecclesiasticus 5:7 Make no tarrying to turn to the Lord, and put not off from day to day: for suddenly shall the wrath of the Lord come forth, and in thy security thou shalt be destroyed, and perish in the day of vengeance.

When you hear this GOSPEL, the same as Christ and the Disciples were teaching, do not delay RETURNING to the Laws, Statues and Commandments. You are gambling with your SOUL, and that is the ultimate LOSS!

Matthew 24:39 And knew not until the flood came, and took them all away; so shall also the coming of the Son of man be.

Many Israelites, who the Kingdom was made will be destroyed in the day of The Most High God. They REJECTED The Most High and are trampling over the BLOOD of Christ.

Acts 1:8 But ye shall receive power, after that the Holy Ghost is come upon you: and ye shall be witnesses unto me both in Jerusalem, and in all Judaea, and in Samaria, and unto the uttermost part of the earth.

Christ did not tell all of the Jews to remain in Jerusalem, only His Disciples and Followers. All of the Jews could have received the Holy Ghost, only if they believed in Christ.

Revelation 14:12 Here is the patience of the saints: here *are* they that keep the commandments of God, and the faith of Jesus.

The Jews who were keeping the Commandments of The Most High God and who BELIEVED in Christ were the only Jews who received the Holy Ghost. Those who claim to have the Holy Ghost on Sunday worship, and do not keep the Commandments of The Most High God are LIARS.

1 John 2:4 He that saith, I know him, and keepeth not his commandments, is a liar, and the truth is not in him.

I did not accuse anybody of being a LIAR. The Most High God did! Do not shoot the messenger!

The BLOOD of The Covenants

Hebrews 8:9 Not according to the covenant that I made with their fathers in the day when I took them by the hand to lead them out of the land of Egypt; because they continued not in my covenant, and I regarded them not, saith the Lord.

The Israelites no longer have to worry about making animal sacrifices, with the animals potentially being sick and broken with maim or scurvy. The Most High God is Holy, and Christ is now that SACRIFICE, which is Holy. It GUARANTEES that The Most High God will not be defiled by the FAULTS of men. If an Israelite man, who is faulty, transgressing against His God and his people, he can use a PERFECT and HOLY sacrifice, RETURN to the Father, and keep His Commandments.

Hebrews 8:10 For this *is* the covenant that I will make with the house of Israel after those days, saith the Lord; I will put my laws into their mind, and write them in their hearts: and I will be to them a God, and they shall be to me a people:

The house of Israel consist of the Northern Kingdom, Ephraim, or Samaria AND the Southern Kingdom, Judah, or Jerusalem. The New Covenant did not include any other nations. The Most High will instill the Laws into the minds of the one-third who REPENTS and RETURNS to him. We are not going to be the same way that we are today.

Zechariah 13:9 And I will bring the third part through the fire, and will refine them as silver is refined, and will try them as gold is tried: they shall call on my name, and I will hear them: I will say, It *is* my people: and they shall say, The LORD *is* my God.

The third part of the Israelites will be purified AND The Most High will put the Laws into our minds. Not only that, but He will also give us POWER!

Revelation 2:26 And he that overcometh, and keepeth my works unto the end, to him will I give power over the nations:

The BLOOD of The Covenants

Those Israelites that keeps the Covenant of The Most High God and FAITH in Christ, we will receive POWER over the nations!

Revelation 2:27 And he shall rule them with a rod of iron; as the vessels of a potter shall they be broken to shivers: even as I received of my Father.

Christ will RULE the other nations with a rod of iron. There will be no feminist movement, no LBGTQ, no Civil Rights, no Gangs, No President or Congress or Supreme Court. Christ will also give the Israelites the SAME POWER that He received from His FATHER.

Hebrews 8:11 And they shall not teach every man his neighbor, and every man his brother, saying, Know the Lord: for all shall know me, from the least to the greatest.

When the Covenant is FULLY completed, ALL the Israelites will know the Law, because our minds will be purged of evil. The Israelites will rule the World when Christ returns. The Most High made the World for the Israelites' sake.

The World Was Made For the Israelites' Sake
When The Most High God delivered the Israelites out of Egypt, he gave them the WORLD! He took lands, destroyed their gods. All nations were made to serve us. Under the New Covenant under Christ, He will give us the world and POWER.

2 Esdras 7:6 There is also another thing; A city is builded, and set upon a broad field, and is full of all good things:

New Jerusalem was built a long time ago, and it will be filled with GOOD things.

Romans 7:12 Wherefore the law *is* holy, and the commandment holy, and just, and good.

Only the Israelites, who are keeping the Laws and the Commandments, are the GOOD THINGS that will be filled in the city that The Most High God has made.

The BLOOD of The Covenants

2 Esdras 7:7 The entrance thereof is narrow, and is set in a dangerous place to fall, like as if there were a fire on the right hand, and on the left a deep water:

However, The Most High God is not going to give them the Kingdom, only if they keep His Laws, Statues, and Commandments.

Matthew 7:13 Enter ye in at the strait gate: for wide *is* the gate, and broad *is* the way, that leadeth to destruction, and many there be which go in there at:

Israelites, who are keeping the God of Abraham, Isaac, and Jacob's Laws, Statues, and Commandments, are entering at the STRAIT or STRICT gate.

Matthew 7:14 Because strait *is* the gate, and narrow *is* the way, which leadeth unto life, and few there be that find it.

Only the RIGHTEOUS will enter the gates into the kingdom. However, very few Hebrews want to walk the strict path. They want to be in the WORLD justifying wickedness, supporting EVIL, when the Israelites are supposed to be walking RIGHTEOUSLY.

Isaiah 5:20 Woe unto them that call evil good, and good evil; that put darkness for light, and light for darkness; that put bitter for sweet, and sweet for bitter!

Whether Israelites deem an act to be RACIST, it is JUDGMENT from The Most High God. He causes destruction to come upon you. The God of Abraham, Isaac, and Jacob is a GOD of LOVE, but not the touchy, feely type of love.

Deuteronomy 32:39 See now that I, *even* I, *am* he, and *there is* no god with me: I kill, and I make alive; I wound, and I heal: neither *is there any* that can deliver out of my hand.

When an Israelites understand the JUDGMENTS of The Most High, then you will understand BECAUSE you TRANSGRESSED His Laws, the EFFECTS are the PUNISHMENT that you receive.

The BLOOD of The Covenants

2 Esdras 7:8 And one only path between them both, even between the fire and the water, so small that there could but one man go there at once.

Not only must you stay on the STRAIT pathway, but dangers of destruction exist when you get off the RIGHTEOUS path. This is a TEST, and you cannot walk it as a GROUP, but each soul must walk this path alone.

2 Esdras 7:9 If this city now were given unto a man for an inheritance, if he never shall pass the danger set before it, how shall he receive this inheritance?

The INHERITANCE belongs to the Israelites, but only those who passes through the narrow passages, or the STRICT, STRAIT path, avoiding the dangers of hell

2 Esdras 7:10 And I said, It is so, Lord. Then said he unto me, Even so also is Israel's portion.

NEW Jerusalem is Israel's Portion.

Revelation 21:2 And I John saw the holy city, new Jerusalem, coming down from God out of heaven, prepared as a bride adorned for her husband.

New Jerusalem is the Holy City. Why are so many Israelites concerning themselves with present-day Jerusalem, when the present Jerusalem will not be part of Jacob's Kingdom?

2 Esdras 7:11 Because for their sakes I made the world: and when Adam transgressed my statutes, then was decreed that now is done.

The Most High God made the WORLD, and all its contents, including the people, for the Israelites' sake.

The BLOOD of The Covenants

When Mercy and the Kingdom Returns to the Sons of Jacob

In The Most High God's anger, He removed His PEACE, MERCY and LOVINGKINDNESS, and He will return to MERCY in His season.

Jeremiah 16:5 For thus saith the LORD, Enter not into the house of mourning, neither go to lament nor bemoan them: for I have taken away my peace from this people, saith the LORD, *even* lovingkindness and mercies.

The Most High God presently has no PEACE, MERCY, or LOVINGKINDNESS for His people, because they are behaving wickedly. They mis-understand His LOVE, but there is no LOVE when you do not the things He commands you to do.

Proverbs 8:17 I love them that love me; and those that seek me early shall find me.

The GOD of Abraham, Isaac, and Jacob LOVES those who LOVES HIM, and His LOVE is not that touchy feely LOVE that you are accustomed.

1 John 5:3 For this is the love of God, that we keep his commandments: and his commandments are not grievous.

Our GOD tells the Israelites, in His BOOK, how to LOVE Him, but your Pastor and those who many of you are listening are telling you how to get into the Kingdom of GOD another way.

John 10:1 Verily, verily, I say unto you, He that entereth not by the door into the sheepfold, but climbeth up some other way, the same is a thief and a robber.

Do not fall for that! You are not on the STRAIT path that Christ tells us that we must walk. Your Pastors are giving you instructions on how to get into the Kingdom through robbery and deceit. You do not have to take my word for it. Do as the Bible commands you. I am simply bringing these scriptures out.

The BLOOD of The Covenants

When The Most High Returns to Mercy

When all the Prophecies in OUR Bible unfolds, then the END will come, and so will the beginning.

Isaiah 14:1 For the LORD will have mercy on Jacob, and will yet choose Israel, and set them in their own land: and the strangers shall be joined with them, and they shall cleave to the house of Jacob.

When The Most High GOD returns to Mercy, He will send His Son, Our Savior, to deliver us out of the hands of Our ENEMIES.

Luke 1:71 That we should be saved from our enemies, and from the hand of all that hate us;

Do not overlook the importance of the Israelites, the so-called Blacks, Hispanics, Native Americans, those of the diaspora, dispersed throughout the Americas, Africa, India, Europe, Asia, and the Islands, those of the Sub-Saharan, and the Trans-Atlantic slave trade, we need to be saved from ALL of our ENEMIES. Those who take from you, and give you what they want you to have, like there religion, the image of their god, and their ways.

Isaiah 14:2 And the people shall take them, and bring them to their place: and the house of Israel shall possess them in the land of the LORD for servants and handmaids: and they shall take them captives, whose captives they were; and they shall rule over their oppressors.

When The Most High returns to mercy, we will take of the nations, who had the Israelites as SLAVES, to be our Servants. They became our servants when the Israelites came out of Egypt,

Leviticus 25:45 Moreover of the children of the strangers that do sojourn among you, of them shall ye buy, and of their families that *are* with you, which they begat in your land: and they shall be your possession.

All of these other nations who are cleaving to the Israelites will become our SERVANTS. The BLOOD of Christ, Him becoming the New High Priest is making way for these things to come.

The BLOOD of The Covenants

Isaiah 14:3 And it shall come to pass in the day that the LORD shall give thee rest from thy sorrow, and from thy fear, and from the hard bondage wherein thou wast made to serve,

The so-called Blacks, Hispanics, and Native Americans who have REPENTED and RETURNED to OUR GOD will finally get REST from all our enemies who have been plotting against us for many years. We will finally be ABSOLUTELY FREE!

Isaiah 14:4 That thou shalt take up this proverb against the king of Babylon, and say, How hath the oppressor ceased! the golden city ceased!

The Israelites will take up a saying against EDOM, the King of Babylon, or the RULERS of the Edomite kingdom. How did your oppression end? It definitely was not voluntarily. Esau always have had their hands against the children of Israel.

Psalms 137:7 Remember, O LORD, the children of Edom in the day of Jerusalem; who said, Rase *it*, rase *it, even* to the foundation thereof.

When The Most High returns to MERCY, He will remember their deeds. They have done so much destruction against the Israelites, they will not be part of the kingdom after their kingdom ends, not even a servant.

Obadiah 1:18 And the house of Jacob shall be a fire, and the house of Joseph a flame, and the house of Esau for stubble, and they shall kindle in them, and devour them; and there shall not be *any* remaining of the house of Esau; for the LORD hath spoken *it*.

When The Most High God returns to MERCY on His children, what do you think He will do to those who have their hands on His children? Esau will be destroyed until there is not one left. Getting angry at the TRUTH only means that you HATE the STRAIT path

Psalms 137:8 O daughter of Babylon, who art to be destroyed; happy *shall he be*, that rewardeth thee as thou hast served us.

The BLOOD of The Covenants

The Most High will pay Edom vengeance for the things that they have done against His children of Israel. He will also give the Israelites POWER to aid in their destruction

Isaiah 14:5 The LORD hath broken the staff of the wicked, *and* the scepter of the rulers.

The Messiah, Christ will come and He will destroy all the world governments. There will only be ONE GOVERNMENT, and Christ will be the KING of KINGS.

Revelation 19:16 And he hath on *his* vesture and on his thigh a name written, KING OF KINGS, AND LORD OF LORDS.

Christ will be KING and LORD in every land. There will be no other government. It is best for those who the COVENANT pertains, the Israelites, to practice the RIGHTEOUS ACTS before entering NEW JERUSALEM.

Judges 5:11 *They that are delivered* from the noise of archers in the places of drawing water, there shall they rehearse the righteous acts of the LORD, *even* the righteous acts *toward the inhabitants* of his villages in Israel: then shall the people of the LORD go down to the gates.

Israel, we MUST take the responsibility upon ourselves to REHEARSE these Laws, Statues and Commandments, so that, when we see NEW JERUSALEM descending down from Heaven, we have RIGHTS to enter into it.

Revelation 22:14 Blessed *are* they that do his commandments, that they may have right to the tree of life, and may enter in through the gates into the city.

If you Israelites are not practicing keeping the Laws, Statues and Commandments now, do you think you will get into the kingdom by saying "the Laws are done away, and by GRACE, you are SAVED?

The BLOOD of The Covenants

Romans 6:1 What shall we say then? Shall we continue in sin, that grace may abound?

The question being asked, should you continue to SIN, because you are under GRACE?

Romans 6:2 God forbid. How shall we, that are dead to sin, live any longer therein?

No, because you have REPENTED, you have LEARNED the Laws while you are under GRACE, and you have learned how to walk on the STRAIT path.

Titus 2:11 For the grace of God that bringeth salvation hath appeared to all men,

Grace should be used for ALL Israelites to get themselves back into order, because many of us did not know that we were under the Law, and under the OLD COVENANT, we all would be worthy of DEATH.

Titus 2:12 Teaching us that, denying ungodliness and worldly lusts, we should live soberly, righteously, and godly, in this present world;

Here is the real kicker; you are not under GRACE, only until an Israelite REPENTS and RETURN to the Law. The Most High and Christ gave us GRACE to give us a time period to LEARN the Law and SIN NO MORE! Is not that being what GRACE is used? Furthermore, GRACE is for those who were under the COVENANT. It excludes everyone else. You cannot be under GRACE without a contract, without owing someone..

Isaiah 14:6 He who smote the people in wrath with a continual stroke, he that ruled the nations in anger, is persecuted, *and* none hindereth.

Edom has continually smitten the Israelites. It does not matter what era. When they came into power, their role was to REMOVE OUR GOD FROM US.

The BLOOD of The Covenants

Isaiah 14:7 The whole earth is at rest, *and* is quiet: they break forth into singing.

Who has the WORLD in turmoil today? When Christ comes, there will be no instigations, no attacks at the border, no theft of property, no sanctions, no LBGTQ, etc.

The BLOOD of The Covenants

Chapter 15: The Beginning

Before Jacob's Kingdom can begin, Esau's Kingdom Must officially end.

Isaiah 60:8 Who *are* these *that* fly as a cloud, and as the doves to their windows?

When Christ returns, He will give the Israelites, the Saints, the same POWER that He received from His Father, and from this precept, it appears that the Israelites will have the power of flight.

Isaiah 60:9 Surely the isles shall wait for me, and the ships of Tarshish first, to bring thy sons from far, their silver and their gold with them, unto the name of the LORD thy God, and to the Holy One of Israel, because he hath glorified thee.

After Esau's world ends, Israelites that are on the Islands will be delivered by ships of Spain. They will also be delivering all the gold and silver that they stole

Isaiah 60:10 And the sons of strangers shall build up thy walls, and their kings shall minister unto thee: for in my wrath I smote thee, but in my favor have I had mercy on thee.

As Hebrews, throughout history have built many of our ENEMIES' kingdoms, they will now be building up Jacob's kingdom. They will be our SERVANTS, because Our GOD has returned to MERCY and will show much FAVOR for the Israelites. When the one-third of Israel has been purified, no man of Israel will be walking out of order. We will live in a perfect kingdom with a perfect GOD.

Isaiah 60:11 Therefore thy gates shall be open continually; they shall not be shut day nor night; that *men* may bring unto thee the forces of the Gentiles, and *that* their kings *may be* brought.

With the NEW POWER that the Israelites have received, they will have no fear of the nations. Our gates will remain open for them to deliver their tribute. All the Gentiles and their leaders will be brought, and they will be given a choice.

Isaiah 60:12 For the nation and kingdom that will not serve thee shall perish; yea, *those* nations shall be utterly wasted.

If these kingdoms do not want to SERVE the Israelites, then they will be destroyed, all of them, including their seeds. The same way the Israelites were given choices in their kingdom to either worship their god or DEATH, these surviving nations will be given the same choice.

Isaiah 60:18 Violence shall no more be heard in thy land, wasting nor destruction within thy borders; but thou shalt call thy walls Salvation, and thy gates Praise.

As I mentioned earlier, there will be rest and peace in the land. There will be no more Esau, who is the master deceiver, the devil.

Isaiah 60:19 The sun shall be no more thy light by day; neither for brightness shall the moon give light unto thee: but the LORD shall be unto thee an everlasting light, and thy God thy glory.

As Christ and the Prophets prophesied that the Sun and the Moon will be darken.

Matthew 24:29 Immediately after the tribulation of those days shall the sun be darkened, and the moon shall not give her light, and the stars shall fall from heaven, and the powers of the heavens shall be shaken:

This Bible is in perfect alignment. The Most High God will provide the Light of the Sun by day and the Light of the Moon by Night.

Isaiah 60:21 Thy people also *shall be* all righteous: they shall inherit the land for ever, the branch of my planting, the work of my hands, that I may be glorified.

The entire one-third who are brough through the fire will all be Keeping the Laws, Statues, and Commandments of the GOD of

The BLOOD of The Covenants

Abraham, Isaac, and Jacob. This is the WORK of The Most High. Although it seems to be impossible for Hebrews to be on the same accord, but it will happen at the hands of The Most High and Christ.

Isaiah 60:22 A little one shall become a thousand, and a small one a strong nation: I the LORD will hasten it in his time.

A little one, or an child of God will become a thousand and also a strong nation. It will make sense for what I will finally conclude.

Seven Women Shall Cleave to One Hebrew Man

When The Most High destroys two-thirds of wicked Israelites, and the one-third remains, at least six out of seven will be women.

Isaiah 4:1 And in that day seven women shall take hold of one man, saying, We will eat our own bread, and wear our own apparel: only let us be called by thy name, to take away our reproach.

Seven women SHALL marry one Hebrew man in Jacob's Kingdom. The Israelite man will not have to provide food or clothing for them. The women will want to be married to a Hebrew man to take away their disapproval, considering most Hebrew women have children but are not married. In the Kingdom, our women will not engage it that activity.

Isaiah 4:2 In that day shall the branch of the LORD be beautiful and glorious, and the fruit of the earth *shall be* excellent and comely for them that are escaped of Israel.

There will be RIGHTEOUSNESS in the Kingdom, and the descendants of Jacob will be beautiful, decked in beautiful garments and all shall be GOOD LOOKING, the one-third who overcame.

Isaiah 4:3 And it shall come to pass, *that he that is* left in Zion, and *he that* remaineth in Jerusalem, shall be called holy, *even* every one that is written among the living in Jerusalem:

All that remain in ZION or New Jerusalem shall have their name written in the Book of Life.

The BLOOD of The Covenants

Isaiah 4:4 When the Lord shall have washed away the filth of the daughters of Zion, and shall have purged the blood of Jerusalem from the midst thereof by the spirit of judgment, and by the spirit of burning.

All the filth that Hebrew women picked up in Esau's kingdom will be washed away by fire and destruction. The Blood of the Jew will be purged by fire and the sword..

Isaiah 66:16 For by fire and by his sword will the LORD plead with all flesh: and the slain of the LORD shall be many.

Two-thirds of Israel will be purged. They do not believe in the GOD of Abraham, Isaac, and Jacob, they hate their brothers, and many of them hate their people.

The Covenant that Christ came to prepare, the New TESTAMENT, He replaced animal sacrifice with a PERFECT sacrifice, using His BLOOD that will allow an Israelite to be forgiven of all sins, except transgressing against the Holy Ghost (**Matthew 12:31**). There is not one scripture that would suggest that Christ deliberately went to speak to the other nations. They spoke with Christ, trying to refute His claims, along with the Elders, the Scribes, Pharisees, and the Chief Priest. Christ is also the New High Priest, who sits next to His Father, asking forgiveness on the behalf of the Israelites. Prior to this New Covenant, the Israelites went without a Mediator for about 450 years, after The Most High fired the Levite Priest. When Christ died, the New Testament was created, which brough forth GRACE, because being without the Law leaves an Israelite at a disadvantage without Grace. You have to have a time period under Grace to learn the Law and understand how to live godly and righteous in the world that you are presently living. An Israelite is not under GRACE, until he or she REPENTS, because The Most High does not hear SINNERS. The New Covenant under Christ is preparing the Israelites for the Kingdom to come. All the Israelites who want to get on the STRAIT path and remain on it, you must, under GRACE learn how to be godly, and live righteously, loving your GOD, and your NEIGHBORS according to the Laws of the God of Abraham, Isaac, and Jacob.

The BLOOD of The Covenants

Printed in Great Britain
by Amazon

22948568R00079